Major Arthur Ormand Norman.
Photograph reproduced by courtesy of The Gordon Highlanders Museum

Captain Jephson George Mignon
Reproduced by kind permission of Digital Preservation Leicestershire, Leicester and Rutland Record Office

Studies in the History of Surrey Schools
Volume 2

STAND AT EASE
The Origins and Systematic Development of Children's Physical Training in the County of Surrey's Public Elementary Schools 1905-1921 Pioneered by Major Arthur Ormand Norman: A Documentary History

by

J Robert Pegg
MA (Ed) History of Education (1870-1939)
MA (Ed) Curriculum Studies
Chairman, Ealing Primary Schools Athletic Association 1996-2003
and Ealing Primary Schools Football Association 1998-2003

The title is taken from:
Board of Education. Syllabus of Physical Exercises for Use in Public Elementary Schools, 26, HMSO, 1904.

abpublishing
Ripley, Surrey

Published by
Angela Blaydon Publishing Ltd
2 Elm Close, Ripley, GU23 6LE
www.abpublishing.com

© J Robert Pegg 2017

ISBN: 978-0-9539821-6-5

All rights reserved. No part of this publication may be reproduced, stored in a retrieval system, or transmitted in any form or by any means, electronic, mechanical, photocopying, recording or otherwise, without prior permission of the Publishers.

Cover design and typesetting
© Angela Blaydon Publishing Ltd

Cover photograph
Leicester Regiment Officers June 1914
© Royal Leicestershire Regimental Archives
and is reproduced by kind permission of Digital Preservation, Leicestershire, Leicester and Rutland Record Office.

Set in Times 10pt
Printed on paper from sustainable sources

Printed by Hobbs the Printers Ltd, Totton, Hants. SO40 3WX
www.hobbs.uk.com

CONTENTS

		Page
List of Illustrations		*iii*
List of Colour Plates		*iii*
Acknowledgements		*iv*
Other Books by the Author		*v*
Abbreviations		*vi*
Preface		*ix*
Chapter 1	Introduction	1
Chapter 2	J.C. Colvill, Colonel Fox and Lord Meath: Architects(?)/Planners(?)/Designers(?) of the Path towards the Model Course	5
Chapter 3	The Report of the Staffing Sub-Committee dd. 14 September 1904	8
Chapter 4	The Interim Report of the Special Committee Cognate	10
Chapter 5	The State of PT in Surrey's Elementary Schools – 21 December 1905	13
Chapter 6	Classes, Certificates and Colonel Fox	18
Chapter 7	Reports of the Superintendent 1906/1907	22
Chapter 8	Further Reports of the Superintendent of PT on Physical Training	24
Chapter 9	More Notes on PT	27
Chapter 10	The Death of Major Norman	31
Chapter 11	The Consultative Board and Sergeant Mills	38
Chapter 12	The Appointment of Captain Mignon as Superintendent of PT	40
Chapter 13	Estimates for 1909/1910	42
Chapter 14	Military Drill and the SEC	44
Chapter 15	The Persistence of the Military Drill Lobby and the Revised 1909 Syllabus	49
Chapter 16	Reformed Sub-Committees	53
Chapter 17	1910 to August 1914	55
Chapter 18	The Death of Lieutenant-Colonel Mignon	58
Chapter 19	1916 and After	62
Chapter 20	Conclusion	65
Appendix I	Lord Meath	69
Appendix II	A Short History of Physical Education from Rousseau to 1904.	73
Appendix III	Overpressure	80
Appendix IV	The Concept of Physical Deterioration	82

Appendix V	Degeneration from the Boer War to 1904	87
Appendix VI	Degeneration-Eugenics	93
Appendix VII	Sir George Malcolm Fox	95
Appendix VIII	Programme of the Display of Physical Training at the Royal Albert Hall Saturday 7 June 1902	98
Appendix IX	A Short Introduction to the Education (Provision of Meals) Act, 1906	102
Appendix X	Memorandum of Physical Training: Practical Suggestions Principally for Rural Schools	103
Appendix XI	A Diary of Sir Lauder Brunton's proposed League for PE and Improvement	105
Appendix XII	Responses to the Appointment of Major Norman	109
Appendix XIII	Attendances at PT Courses & Certificates awarded and Inspections made by Colonel Fox	112
Appendix XIV	A Biography of Captain F H Grenfell and his views on Swedish Gymnastics	114
Appendix XV	BSA Advertisement on Rifle Practice	124
Appendix XVI	Arthur Wakefield Chapman	125
Appendix XVII	Dorothy Le Couteur-Organiser of PT	126
Appendix XVIII	SCC-Managers' Handbook 1912-The PT Curriculum	135
Appendix XIX	Elementary Education in Surrey 1903 (This appendix appears as Chapter 2 in "In Sickness and In Health")	137
Bibliography		140

LIST OF ILLUSTRATIONS

Major Arthur Ormand Norman	Frontispiece
Captain Jephson George Mignon	Frontispiece
Major Norman and the Gordon Highlanders	33
Major Norman and the Gordon Highlanders	34
Major Norman and the Gordon Highlanders	35
Major Norman and the Gordon Highlanders	36
Lieutenant Colonel J G Mignon	59
Leicestershire Regiment Officers 9th Btn	60
Lord Meath	70
Lord Meath	71
Lads' Drill Association Programme of the Display of Physical Training at the Royal Albert Hall 7 June 1902	98
Lads' Drill Association Programme	99
Lads' Drill Association Programme	100
Lads' Drill Association Programme - Publicity	101
F H Grenfell	118
F H Grenfell	119
HMS Penshurst	120
F H Grenfell Death Certificate	121
Sculpture by F H Grenfell	122
BSA Advertisement on Rifle Practice	124
Photograph from Tolkein's Gedling	131
School inspector Dorothy Le Couteur	132
Sir George Newman and Miss Le Couteur 1930	133

LIST OF COLOUR PLATES

Plate I.   *The Grave of Major Norman in Haslemere Cemetery*
Plate II.   *Lieutenant Colonel Mignon*
Plate III.   *Lieutenant Colonel Mignon*
Plate IV.   *Lieutenant Colonel Mignon*
Plate V.   *Officers of the 8th Battalion, The Leicestershire Regisment*
Plate VI.   *The 8th Leicestershire Regisment*
Plate VII.   *The 8th Leicestershire Regiment*
Plate VIII.   *Thiepval Memorial, Thiepval*
Plate IX.   *Map of the Battle of Bazentin Ridge*
Plate X.   *Colonel Fox*
Plate XI.   *Colonel Fox*
Plate XII.   *Colonel Fox in Vanity Fair*
Plate XIII.   *Fox's endorsement of this "little book" as a guide to the 1904 syllabus*
Plate XIV.   *German shrapnel from UB-37*
Plate XV.   *Written account of shrapnel incident on 14 January 1917 by Captain Grenfell.*
Plate XVI.   *Tolkien's 1911 Journey*

ACKNOWLEDGEMENTS

My grateful thanks to the staff at the Surrey History Centre in Woking for allowing the use of original documents of the Dorking British (Powell-Corderoy) School to be published and their generous help in making this book possible.

My thanks also to Mrs Evelyn Cowie who supervised my dissertation on The Impact of Contemporary and Historical Influences on Aspects of Physical Education In Elementary Schools In Surrey 1894-1930 as part fulfilment of the requirements for the degree of Master of Arts (Education) at King's College, University of London in 1985. This book represents an extension of the information and ideas expressed in that dissertation.

My gratitude is also due to Christopher Nixon for his investigative help in the biographies of individuals mentioned in the book and for his invaluable help in clarifying some of the more complicated computer procedures.

My grateful thanks to the following schools for allowing me to view their log books for the original dissertation: The Hythe Schools, Staines; Godalming National School, Godalming; Stepgates School, Chertsey; Goldsworth School, Woking; Manorcroft Schools, Egham; St Ann's Heath School, Virginia Water; Clandon C of E (Aided) Infant School, West Clandon.

I would also thank the following schools in Surrey for their willingness to reply to my letter 20 June 2014: Tillingbourne Junior School, Guildford; Sandfield Primary School, Guildford; Cranleigh C of E Primary School, Cranleigh; Epsom Primary School, Epsom; St James C of E Primary School, Weybridge; Stepgates Community School, Chertsey; The Hythe School, Staines; Wonersh and Shenley Green C of E Aided Primary School, Guildford. Powell-Corderoy, Dorking; Godalming School, Godalming; Goldsworth School, Woking.

My thanks also to Andrew H Morton for his kind permission to publish photographs in his collection

Rosemary Moon @ nwkcollege.ac.uk at the Bergman Osterberg Union (BOU) Archive for permission to publish the photograph of Sir George Newman and Dorothy Le Couteur.

Glenn Asher Gordon, Digital Preservation, Leicester and Rutland Record Office, Long Street, Wigston Magna, LE18 2AH.

Philip R French, Curator of the Royal Leicestershire Regimental Archives

Charles Reid, Gordon Highlanders Museum for the provision of photographs of Major Norman and to his recommendations for revised aspects of his military career.

Modern Records Centre, University Library, University of Warwick for permission to publish a photograph of Lord Meath and the State University of Queensland.

Frank Grenfell, nephew of Francis H Grenfell, for permission to publish information and photographs supplied by him relating to his uncle Francis H Grenfell.

Greg Witt @alpenwild.com for the preparation of a map relating to the possible route of J R R Tolkien's journey to Switzerland in 1911.

Any faults are the fault of the author only.

OTHER BOOKS BY THE AUTHOR

This book is one of a series of three dealing with elements of the educational history of the Surrey Educational Committee between the Education Acts of 1902 and 1921:

"In Sickness and in Health" The Origins and Systematic Development of Children's Medical Inspection and Treatment in the County of Surrey's Public Elementary Schools 1905-1921 Pioneered by Dr Thomas Henry Jones: A Documentary History. Vol. 1.

"In the Swim" The Origins and Systematic Development of Children's Swimming in the County of Surrey's Public Elementary Schools 1905-1921 Pioneered by Major Arthur Ormand Norman: A Documentary History. Vol. 3.

~~~~~~~~~~~~

The following book traces the origin and development of after-school activities in sport in Croydon's Public Elementary Schools through the medium of local newspapers from 1893-1910.

Quick March to Athletic Sports: The Origins and Development of Drill, Athletics, Cricket, Football and Swimming in Croydon's Public Elementary Schools 1893-1910: A Newspaper, Documentary History.

ABBREVIATIONS

1870 Act	The Elementary Education Act, 1870
1893 Act	The Elementary Education (Blind and Deaf Children) Act, 1893
1899 Act	Elementary Education (Defective and Epileptic Children) Act, 1899
1902 Act	The Education Act, 1902
1903 Report	Report of the Royal Commission on Physical Training (Scotland), 1903
1904 Report	Inter-Departmental Committee on Physical Deterioration, 1904
1904 Syllabus	Syllabus of Physical Exercises for use in Public Elementary Schools, 1904, Circular 515, 22 August 1904
1905 Report	Inter-Departmental Committee on Medical Inspection and Feeding of Children Attending Public Elementary Schools, 1905
1905 Syllabus	Syllabus of Physical Exercises for Use in Public Elementary Schools, 1905
1906 Act	Education (Provision of Meals) Act, 1906
1907 Act	Education (Administrative Provisions) Act, 1907.
1909 Syllabus	The Syllabus of Physical Exercises for Public Elementary Schools, 1909
1918 Act	Education Act, 1918
AD	Anno Domini
BA	Bachelor of Arts
BC	Before Christ
BMJ	British Medical Journal
Board	Board of Education
Boer War	South African Wars (1897-1902)
CA	Chartered Accountant
C of E	Church of England
circular 515	Circular 515
CMO	Chief Medical Officer
code(s)	Day Code of Regulations
DD	Doctor of Divinity
D Sc.	Doctor of Science
DSO	Distinguished Service Order
Education Department	Committee of Council on Education
EMO	Education Medical Officer
HMI	His/Her Majesty's Inspector

JP	Justice of the Peace
KCB	Knight Commander of the Order of Bath
Lea(s)	Local Education Authorities
LL D	Doctor of Laws
MA	Master of Arts
MD/Dr	Medical Doctor
Memorandum 1901	Memorandum of the Departmental Committee on Training College Courses of Instruction, 1901
MI	Medical Inspection
MIPTS	Medical Inspection and Physical Training Sub-Committee
MO	Medical Officer
Model Course	A Model Course of Physical Training for Use in the Upper Departments of Public Elementary Schools, 1902, Circular 452, 20 June 1901
MP	Member of Parliament
NUT	National Union of Teachers
OBE	Order of the British Empire
p.a.	per annum
PC	Privy Council, Counsellor
PE	Physical Education
PES	Public Elementary Schools
PT	Physical Training
PT Memorandum	Memorandum on Physical Training Practical Suggestions for Rural Schools
RGO	Registrar General
RIPH	Royal Institute of Public Health
RN	Royal Navy
SCC	Surrey County Council
SEC	Surrey Education Committee
SHC	Surrey History Centre
SMO	School Medical Officer
SMS	School Medical Service
Suggestions	Handbook of Suggestions for the Use of Teachers and Others concerned in the work of Elementary Schools, 1905 & Subsequent years
TNA	The National Archives
TUC	Trades Union Congress
UB	Undersea Boat

PREFACE

This book is dedicated to the memories of Major Arthur Ormand Norman and Captain J.G. Mignon, later Lieutenant-Colonel, who, as Superintendents of Physical Training in the Public Elementary Schools of Surrey between 1905 and 1916 dedicated their lives to the concept of Swedish Drill in the physical training of the teachers and children of Surrey's Public Elementary Schools.

Both had served in the Boer War. Major Norman died in the service of the Elementary schools through overwork while Lieutenant-Colonel Mignon lost his life in the service of his country during the First World War.

Trench Duty

Shaken from sleep, and numbed and scarce awake,
Out in the trench with three hours' watch to take,
I blunder through the splashing mirk; and then
Hear the gruff muttering voices of the men
Crouching in cabins candle-chinked with light.
Hark! There's the big bombarbment on our right
Rumbling and bumping; and the dark's glare
Of flickering horror in the sectors where
We raid the Boche; men waiting, stiff and chilled,
Or crawling on their bellies through the wire.
"What? Stretcher-bearers wanted? Someone killed?"
Five minutes ago I heard a sniper fire:
Why did he do it?...Starlight overhead –
Blank stars. I'm wide-awake; and some chap's dead.

Siegfried Sassoon

Gardner, Brian, *Up The Line To Death: The War Poets 1914-1918*, 1964, 130/131; An Anthology Methuen, 2007 edition.

CHAPTER 1
INTRODUCTION

The Education Act 1902 (1902 Act), like The Elementary Education Act 1870 (1870 Act) before it, did not include any reference to the health and welfare of the elementary school child. Attempts had been made to deal with certain children with special needs through The Elementary Education (Blind and Deaf) Children Act 1893 (1893 Act) and the Elementary Education (Defective and Epileptic) Act 1899 (1899 Act), but the vast majority of children in the Public Elementary Schools (PES) remained outside the web of health and welfare provision.

Matters came to a head with the problems of recruitment for the South African War, 1899-1902, (Boer War). Of 11,000 men, who had volunteered from Manchester in 1899, only 3,000 were physically fit. Of those only 1,000 satisfied army standards, the remaining 2,000 being relegated to the militia.[1]

Reginald Brabazon, 12th Earl of Meath[2], (1841-1929 – *see* Appendix I) was a long-standing critic of urban life, to which the population of England was increasingly drawn. Cities and towns were crowded, lacking in air and did not have the proper means for providing exercise.[3] Meath, a liberal imperialist, and a supporter of the Boer War, had campaigned long and vigorously for the inclusion of physical exercise into the curriculum of the PES.[4] (For a short history of Physical Education (PE) *see* Appendix II; for the concept of Overpressure in PES I *see* Appendix III)

Many people, he declared, did not have wholesome or, even, necessary food, warmth or clothing[5]. The lines of the Roman poet, Juvenal, (60-140AD), he quoted,

"Mens sana in corpore sano"[6]

were as valid in the aggregate as they were of the individual.[7] Fresh air, exercise and gymnastics were necessary for the children attending all Board Schools. (for an explanation of Board Schools *see* end notes)

If this was an appeal for curriculum reform, it was also an invocation to an imperial destiny. Yet, paradoxically, it contained the fearful voice of Social Darwinism; that the British race, was, through rapid, unplanned urbanisation, deteriorating and degenerating both physically and mentally. (Appendices IV, V, VI)

Curriculum reform meant adaptation. Adaptation meant a glorious future. Failure to reform would ensure the further deterioration of the physiological impulse of the human species in its urban context. More specifically, the British race itself would be unable to fulfil its destined role in world affairs. By 1902, the view of the Imperialists was that the restoration of military drill was, therefore, necessary to prevent physiological deterioration and to prepare the children of the PES for their destiny as imperial auxiliaries to the middle and upper classes.[8]

Meath aligned himself with certain members of the educational establishment. One of Her Majesty's Inspectors (HMI), J C Colvill from Surrey gave evidence to a Departmental Committee on Physical Training. Published as a *Memorandum of the Departmental Committee* on *Training College Courses of Instruction 1901*, (Memorandum 1901), he considered that military drill ought to be included in the concept of Physical Training (PT).[9]

Subsequently, *A Model Course of Physical Training for Use in the Upper Departments of Public Elementary Schools 1902*, (Model Course) was issued.[10]

Colonel George Malcolm Fox, (1843-1918 – Appendix VII), who had been appointed by the Board as Inspector of Physical Training to implement the Model Course[11] had close personal relations with both Meath and Colvill. On a visit to the Dorking British School on 28 April 1902, Colvill had suggested to Mr. Cousins, the headmaster, that the school should enter a display of PT which was to be held at the Royal Albert Hall on 7 June 1902 (Appendix VIII). On 1 May 1902, Colonel Fox returned to the school with Mr. Colvill and selected the first class as one of the squads to appear at the Royal Albert Hall.[12] On the front page of *The Dorking & Leatherhead Advertiser* of 7 June 1902 an advertisement announcing the Annual Festival of the Dorking British School noted that forty-eight boys and girls from the school were to take part in the display with eleven other schools on that day and that the display was to be repeated on 11 June at the annual festival at Pippabrook House, the home of Mrs. Aggs.

The display was held under the auspices of the Lads' Drill Association, which had been founded in 1901 by Lord Meath,[13] President of the Association. The exercises performed were taken from the 1902 Model Course.[14] In the presence of the Prince and Princess of Wales, Meath viewed the display as an important step in the growth of an association which aimed at nothing less than a revolution in the system of elementary education![15]

Meath promoted the Model Course for all elementary schools as a compulsory entitlement. Accordingly, the government's responsibility was to recognise the necessity for the Model Course, and, therefore, should ensure adequate training of students in training colleges and of established teachers as instructors without unfair expense to themselves. Training courses should consequently reward these instructors with a certificate. Skilled direction and supervision in PT should, therefore, be provided by the education authorities.[16]

In spite of Meath's enthusiasm, however, there was a general antipathy to the Model Course.[17] Paragraph 3 of the *Report of the Inter-Departmental Committee on the Model Course of Physical Exercises*, 1904 (Command 2032) stated:

> "we do not consider the 'Model Course' to be a suitable course for use in schools, in part because certain of the exercises included in the course seem... unsuitable as elements of a compulsory course, but chiefly because the course as a whole does not seem to be constructed on well-defined general principles educed from a consideration of the function of physical exercise as a necessary element in a well-ordered course of general education for children."

Some of those most antipathetic came from a series of articles in the Manchester Guardian which were later collectively published in *National Physical Training, An Open Debate*, 1904. Winston Churchill (1874-1965) and other contributors suggested a series of remedies including the feeding of school children, the implementation of a system of Swedish Drill and school medical inspection (MI).[18]

Meath's obsession was, in a sense, a general obsession with a presumed deterioration of the British race[19] as a result of Britain's performance in the Boer War.[20] So, although Meath and his followers were, in a sense, attuned to the sense of change needed in respect of the physical education of the elementary school child, their solution was based on an insufficiently visionary sense of what the purpose of a PES was in respect of the development of the potential and capacities of each and every individual child in a developing democratic society.

One sense of change had begun with the 1902 Act. The *Code* (code) of 1904 – codes were the mechanism through which the curriculum of the elementary schools was regulated on a year by year basis – was, for the first time, also issued in general form as the *Handbook of Suggestions for the Use of Teachers and Others concerned in the work of Public Elementary Schools 1905*, (Suggestions). The architect of both these measures was Robert Laurie Morant (1863-1920), permanent secretary at the Board of Education (Board).[21]

In spite of the fact that the 1902 Act had not addressed the problem of health and welfare, nevertheless, the auguries concerning changes were beginning to make some impact in the code of 1904, the Suggestions of 1905 and various pressure groups, such as the Royal Institute of Public Health (RIPH), which urged the Board to appoint a permanent medical officer (MO) to advise it on medical matters.[22]

Alfred Eichholz, Doctor of Medicine (MD/Dr.), (1863-1933), had been appointed in 1898 as an HMI, but, as the one and only medical inspector at the Board.[23] His responsibilities as the medical director at the Board were for defective and epileptic children alone since no legislation existed for the health and welfare of the mass of children educated in the PES. Advice and direction, the RIPH argued, could be given to a school with the appointment of such a figure at the Board on such topics as ventilation, lighting and the kinds of desk in use, on the closure of schools owing to epidemics of infectious diseases and grants relative to such closures.

Morant thought that the RIPH interest was a cool interference in the administration of the Board[24] and rejected the idea of a special MO or that the creation of a special department was either necessary or expedient.[25]

Nevertheless, a series of governmental reports were to be influential in changes which were to considerably alter the status of the elementary school child in terms of his/her health and welfare. They were: *The Report of the Royal Commission on Physical Training (Scotland) 1903*, (1903 Report), *The Inter-Departmental Committee on Physical Deterioration 1904*, (1904 Report) and the *Inter-Departmental Committee on Medical Inspection and Feeding of Children Attending Public Elementary Schools 1905*, (1905 Report).

Three subsequent Acts of Parliament contributed to the health and welfare condition of the elementary school child: the Education (Provision of Meals) Act 1906, (1906 Act) (Appendix IX) later reinforced by the Education (Provisionof Meals) Act 1914. A further Education (Administrative Provisions) Act 1907, (1907 Act) established the School Medical Service (SMS) from 1 January 1908 with (later Sir) George Newman (1870-1948) as Chief Medical Officer (CMO).

As a result of the 1903, and particularly the 1904 Report, the Board issued *Circular 515* (circular 515) on 22 August 1904. Accompanying circular 515 was the *Syllabus of Physical Exercises for use in Public Elementary Schools 1904*, (1904 Syllabus), which was based on the *Swedish System of Exercises* or drill as it was commonly called.

Surrey County Council (SCC) in the guise of its educational administration, the Surrey Education Committee (SEC), was in the vanguard of the changes envisaged in circular 515 concerning the implementation of MI and Physical Training.

Notes

1. Curtis, S J., MA., Ph.D. & Boultwood, M E A., MA. *An Introductory History of English Education since 1800*, 168, University Tutorial Press Ltd., London, 4th Edition 1970, First Published 1960.

2. Penn, Alan. *Targeting Schools, Drill, Militarism and Imperialism*, 67-75, Woburn Press, London, 1999.
3. Meath, Earl. 'Health and Physique of our City Populations', in Meath, Earl. *Prosperity or Pauperism*, 5, Longmans Green & Co., London, 1888.
4. Ibid.
5. Ibid.
6. Juvenal. *The Sixteen Satires*, 104 AD, 217, translated by Peter Green, Penguin, Harmondsworth, 1967.
7. Meath, Earl. op. cit, 2.
8. Penn, Alan. op. cit., 166-7.
9. Committee on Training College Courses of Instruction, *Memorandum of the Departmental Committee on Training College Courses of Instruction*, 1901, Volume 1, evidence of J C Colvill, 24 April 1901, pp. 183-7, Minutes of Evidence 4575-4666. HMSO.
10. TNA. ED 142/39, Board of Education, issued to HMIs, Circular 452, dd. 20 June 1901, Day School Code, Schedule III, (This circular enclosed the initial printed version – in Print Form only – of the Model Course.)
11. McIntosh, Peter. *Physical Education In England Since 1800*, 1952, 148, Bell & Hyman Ltd., London, Revised and Enlarged Edition 1968.
12. Surrey History Centre. (SHC), C/ES/115/2/1/1, Log Book, Dorking British School, 261.
13. Penn, Alan. op. cit., 84-5.
14. SHC. op. cit., C/ES/115/2/1/1, 263.
15. *The Times*, 9 June, 1902, 10
16. Ibid.
17. McIntosh, Peter, op. cit., 145; *see also* May, J. Curriculum Development Under the School Board for London: Physical Education, 1971, 101-104, Unpublished Ph. D. Thesis, University of Leicester, 1971.
18. Atkins, J B., *National Physical Training, An Open Debate*, 151, Ibister and Company, London, 1904.
19. *The Times*, op. cit., 10.
20. Ibid.
21. Curtis, S J., MA., Ph.D. & Boultwood, M E A., MA., op. cit, 162-79.
22. TNA, ED 23/198, letter dated 4 February 1903, from RIPH.
23. Aldrich, Richard & Gordon, Peter. *Dictionary of British Educationists*, 77, Woburn Press, London, 1989.
24. TNA, ED 23/198, op. cit., letter dated 3 July 1903.
25. Ibid.

Note: Board Schools were those schools which were provided and managed by a School Board which had been established by the 1870 Act. By the 1902 Act all Public Elementary Schools were divided into provided and non-provided schools. Non-provided schools were those commonly known as voluntary schools, i.e. denominational schools. PES, previously classified as Board Schools under the 1870 Act, were subsequently recognised as provided schools under the 1902 Act. Both Provided and Non-Provided schools came under the administrative control of Local Education Authorities (Lea[s]) under the 1902 Act.

CHAPTER 2
J.C. COLVILL, COLONEL FOX AND LORD MEATH: ARCHITECTS(?)/PLANNERS(?)/DESIGNERS(?) OF THE PATH TOWARDS THE MODEL COURSE

A newspaper article[1] shortly after the publication of the Memorandum 1901,[2] gives some indication of the way Colvill, Fox and Meath were trying to manoeuvre a position in respect of the military drill they envisaged as a developmental system of physical exercises in the PES, which resulted in the issue of the Model Course.

The article, entitled *Physical Exercise in Schools-An Interesting Exhibition* declared that many teachers had difficulty in finding a really practical system of physical exercises to introduce to their children, the existing systems being unable to meet the needs of the case.

On Friday 28 June 1901, the day before the article was published, hundreds of teachers from the Guildford area met in the headquarter's gymnasium of the Aldershot Barracks. An exhibition of PT, arranged by Colonel Fox, Inspector of Army Gymnasia, *at the request of J C. Colvill*, was given by the regimental schools. Amongst the assembled throng was Lord Meath, Sir Henry Craik, (1846-1927 – head of the Scottish Education Department), General Sir Frederick Maurice* (1871-1951), A.W. Chapman JP, CA, (Chairman of the SEC – Appendix XVI), and numerous others.

The purpose of the display was to show the progress of PT from infants to grown men. The first display was a class of infants from the Model School, Aldershot (which may betray the origins of the title of the Model Course) under the direction of Miss Cattley, their mistress. The infants went through a series of exercises with dumb-bells to musical accompaniment.

On the completion of their display, one child was retained, and, under the direction of Sergeant-Instructor Pattison went through a special drill for which she received a large doll in recognition of the perfection of her display. All of the children received a box of chocolates because they had sacrificed part of their holiday to show the display.

After the infants came some boys. Their drill included marching, exercise of the feet, the knees, on hips and chests expanded and hopping and running with knees up.

Older girls followed with a similar routine but adapted to make it suitable for girls.

Next came a company of boys from King Edward's School, Witley, who were carrying dummy rifles, marched to the music of the school band and performed a more complicated routine than previously seen.

Subsequently perfection was reached with the physical exercises performed by the Army Instructors' Class.

---

*   *See* Appendix XI for the role that General Maurice played in the formation of the National League for PE and Improvement in 1905 initiated by Sir Lauder Brunton. (Chapter 14.)

Between each of the displays, Colonel Fox remarked that the object was not to make soldiers but to make the children healthy, and bring them up in habits of discipline. Physical Training, he said, affected the mind even more than the body. With this in mind, it is difficult to understand why Fox was apparently not only in favour of a military style display but also the 1901 Syllabus. Perhaps, at this stage he was convinced of the benefits of a military style drill for school children, although he seems later to have changed his mind and embraced the Swedish System. Nevertheless his attempts to introduce it into the army were apparently thwarted. (*see* Appendix VII)

Lord Meath and Sir Henry Craik pointed out the responsibilities that fell upon the teachers as trainers of future generations and the important part which really systematic training could play in educational work, with Craik praising Colvill in complimentary terms.

Almost a year later[3] the annual Guildford Educational Conference for teachers and managers of Colvill's district embracing a large part of Surrey and Sussex was again held at the Borough Halls, Guildford.

Colvill congratulated teachers for their past year's work on PT which had been introduced into the curriculum last year. Six-hundred and seventy-seven teachers had attended special classes, mostly at their own expense. (*see* infra Chapter 5, Note 5 TNA Ed. 24/37A).

Referring to the display at the Royal Albert Hall, the previous Saturday, which experts had told him was amongst the best there, he observed that the War Office had just issued an order by which Army Gymnasium Instructors should be everywhere put at the disposal of teachers' classes. The Lads' Drill Association was applying to the War Office for gymnasium superintendents to sign certificates for those teachers who showed themselves reasonably good at directing a class. Unfortunately, the certificates would not be issued by the Board of Education, as they were in Scotland by the Scottish Education Department. Nevertheless, certificates would be issued by competent instructors of the Association. However, he had not given up hope that the Board would issue its own certificates.

One month later, a letter appeared[4] in *The Times* from Lord Meath, which was headed Physical Training in Schools. It observed that a general order had been issued by the War Office dated 2 July 1902 under the authority of Field Marshall, Lord Frederick Roberts. Meath noted that the Adjutant-General to the Forces had drawn the attention of general officers commanding divisions, to the fact that the Board and the War Office, had, after consultation, proposed a model course of physical training for schools under its jurisdiction, at the suggestion of the Lads' Drill Association.

Roberts had approved facilities for educational authorities or school managers who wished to employ qualified non-commissioned officers at the Army School of Gymnastics to be used at any established or modified gymnasia or selected centre for the course to be undertaken. The classes were to be of twenty to thirty people with a charge of about 3d. per lesson per hour being appropriate. Meath observed that the cause of physical education was enhanced by such training and hoped that an arrangement for the awarding of certificates would be possible from a recognised authority in the future.

Approximately three weeks later *The Times*[5] reported that a *Memorandum On Physical Training, Practical Suggestions, Principally for Rural Schools* (PT memorandum – Appendix X) concerning PT had been issued by the Board. It contained suggestions, mainly for rural schools, designed to help teachers and managers carry out the requirements of Schedule III of the code because of difficulties experienced in small country schools. Noting that the ordinary school staff should normally do the teaching of PT, nevertheless groups of schools could come together to secure the services of a qualified instructor trained in the Army Gymnastics Course.

Reiterating much of the letter from Meath, managers who wished to avail themselves of these facilities were to apply to the general officer commanding of the district in which the schools were situated, a list of which was given at the end of this PT memorandum. This memorandum was undated and also contained a copy of the letter dated 2 July 1902 and signed by J.K. Kenny, Adjutant-General to the Forces.

Notes

1. *The Surrey Times*, 29 June 1901, 5.
2. supra, Chapter 1.
3. *The Surrey Times*, 21 June 1902, 6.
4. *The Times*, 23 July 1902, 11.
5. Ibid, 16 August 1902, 2.

CHAPTER 3
THE REPORT OF THE STAFFING SUB-COMMITTEE
DATED 14 SEPTEMBER 1904

The chairman of the Staffing Sub-Committee, A.W. Chapman, reported on PT, one of the cognate considerations posited by circular 515[1]. The Staffing Sub-Committee recognised both the moral and physical significance of physical exercises mentioned in the circular. Recommending that copies of circular 515 and the 1904 Syllabus be obtained and forwarded to schools, it suggested that managers should subsequently report on:

(a) the systematized course of instruction in use at the school which was not to include boys' drill
(b) whether or not the course in the school could be integrated with the 1904 Syllabus, and, if so, whether such a transition would be gradual
(c) if no course of instruction was in force in the school, whether or not the managers would adopt the 1904 Syllabus without further delay. If they did, was any member of staff capable of giving instruction in physical exercises?

In this regard and for the success of the scheme, the Sub-Committee recognised that some form of proper instruction and training for teachers was necessary, especially in the more rural parts of the county. However, such instruction could not be dealt with by the Elementary Committee according to the terms of Section 22(3) of the 1902 Act which read:

"The power to supply or aid the supply of education other than elementary includes a power to train teachers, and to supply or aid the supply of any education except where that education is given at a public elementary school."[2]

Nevertheless, it seems clear that the questions posed by the Staffing Sub-Committee were directly attributable to the necessary conditions imposed by the Board, whose regulations, provided for a course of instruction with the provision that a graduated scheme for teaching be submitted to, and approved by the inspector.[3]

It, therefore followed, that, if PT was to be properly carried out throughout the county (*see* Appendix XIX for the number of Elementary schools there were in Surrey in 1903), it was essential to institute a system of PT, instruction and inspection by competent, qualified staff. Instructors would train teachers at evening or Saturday classes at suitable centres and to give instruction in schools that have no staff qualified to do so. They would also act as Inspectors of all PT given at all elementary and secondary schools in their respective areas.

The Staffing Sub-Committee envisaged four instructors/inspectors would be needed, the cost to be apportioned by the SEC. Nevertheless, financial considerations prevented such appointments in the current financial year but ought to be implemented upon the commencement of the next financial year.[4]

The Elementary Sub-Committee acting upon the recommendation of the Staffing Sub-Committee subsequently recommended to the SEC the necessity of the coordination of the Higher and Elementary Committees so that a system of PT could be implemented on a practical basis.[5]

In the event, the Interim Report of the Special Committee Cognate reported on 1 February 1905.

Notes

1. SHC, Appendix E 6, Report of the Staffing Sub-Committee, dd. 14 September 1904, pp. 1350-2 in Report of the Elementary Sub-Committee, pp. 1227-41, 1240 in *8th Report of the SEC*, 8 November 1904, pp. 1205-1414.
2. Drury, J F W., M.A. *Drury's Manual of Education*, 200, John Heywood, Manchester 2003.
3. SHC, op. cit., Appendix E6, pp.1350-2.
4. SHC, Ibid.
5. SHC, Report of the Elementary Sub-Committee, pp. 1227-41, 1238-40, in op. cit., *8th Report of the SEC*.

CHAPTER 4
THE INTERIM REPORT OF
THE SPECIAL COMMITTEE COGNATE

The Interim Report of the Special Committee Cognate considered both questions of MI and PT posed by circular 515.[1] In addition to the eleven members appointed with A W. Chapman as chairman, J C Colvill and Dr Edward Cox Seaton[2] joined the committee at its inaugural meeting.[3]

As well as considering circular 515, the Special Committee Cognate also reflected upon the Report of the Elementary Committee[4] as well as the Report of the Staffing Committee[5] and the 1904 Report.

PHYSICAL TRAINING

In reflecting upon PT, the Special Committee Cognate resolved:

(a) that the SEC be recommended to adopt the 1904 Syllabus for general use in all SEC schools
(b) that the 1904 Syllabus be gradually adopted.[6]

The Special Committee Cognate also studied returns from schools showing approximate numbers of PT in the elementary schools. The returns showed:

(a)	the number of departments (infant, junior girls, junior boys, etc.) with PT in the curriculum	415
(b)	the number of departments with no PT in the curriculum	32
(c)	the number of departments in which the existing syllabus was adaptable	348
(d)	the number of departments in which gradual transition was recommended	67
(e)	the number of teachers accustomed to giving instruction in the syllabus	1,252
(f)	the number of teachers unqualified and requiring instruction	800

As a result of these statistics, the Special Committee Cognate resolved that it was premature to recommend any comprehensive scheme or wholesale organisation of elementary schools until a properly, technical skilled instructor was appointed for the purpose. It further resolved to appoint only one whole time Superintendent of PT at a salary not exceeding £200 p.a. with travelling expenses. Initially the appointment was to be for one year only.

The officer (sic) appointed, should, in the first instance, make an inspection of the elementary schools and report back on the following points:

(a) the number of schools that required supervision in the adaptation of the existing syllabus to the 1904 Syllabus;
(b) the number of schools that required supervision in starting the 1904 Syllabus;
(c) the probable number of centres required for the instruction of teachers;
(d) a general scheme of organisation for developing and carrying out the the system throughout the county.

The Special Committee Cognate would present the findings above in the form of an interim report and redefine in a further report what new developments were required, especially in regard to adaptations for the secondary schools and the subsequent apportionment of costs between Higher and elementary education.

The Special Committee Cognate estimated an expenditure of £300 commencing 1 April 1905. However, the Committee recommended an additional amount of £400 be included in the estimates in case the Superintendent's initial report necessitated further expenditure.[7]

It was further resolved by the Committee that the Part III authorities (*see* below) be invited to take part in the proposed scheme of instruction and inspection of PT and the scheme of MI and certification in schools under their authority upon terms to be settled between them and the SEC.

The SEC subsequently approved the appointments of Dr. Thomas Henry Jones as Education Medical Officer (EMO) and of Major Arthur Ormand Norman as Superintendent of PT.[8] (For reaction to Major Norman's appointment *see* Appendix XII).

The Surrey Educational Conference opened on Friday 7 July 1905 at the Surbiton Assembly Rooms. In the opening address, A W. Chapman, chairman of both the SEC and the Special Committee Cognate, introduced Dr. Jones and Major Norman to the assembled audience, the purpose of which was to make them known to the managers and teachers employed in Surrey's schools.[9]

Note: Part III Authorities

Section I of the 1902 Act states that for the purpose of this Act the council of every county and of every county borough shall be the local education authority: Provided that the council of a borough with a population of over 10,000, or of an urban district with a population of over 20,000, shall, as respects that borough or district, be the local education authority for the purpose of Part III of this Act, and for that purpose as respects that borough or district, the expression "local education authority" means the council of that borough or district.

Section 5 states: Part III Elementary Education:

Powers and Duties as to Elementary Education
The local education authority shall throughout their area have the powers and duties of a school board and school attendance committee under the Elementary Education Acts, 1870 to 1900, and any other Acts, including local Acts, and shall also be responsible for and have the control

of all secular instruction in public elementary schools not provided by them, and school boards and school attendance committees shall be abolished.

Notes

1. SHC, Appendix E 1, dd 1 February 1905, Interim Report of the Special Committee to consider the Two Cognate Questions of Physical Training and Medical Inspection, pp. 687-93 in *10th Report of the SEC*, 9 May 1905, pp. 557-728.
2. *The Surrey Times*, 30 July 1910, 6; *The Times*, 22 February 1915, 10; (*See* Pegg, J.R. *In Sickness and In Health: The Origins and Systematic Development of Children's Medical Inspection and Treatment in the County of Surrey's Public Elementary Schools 1905-1921, pioneered by Dr Thomas Henry Jones, A Documentary History, Volume 1*)
3. SHC, Appendix E 1, d. 1 February 1905, op. cit., *10th Report of the SEC*.
4. SHC, Report of the Elementary Committee, pp. 600-13, 602, ibid., *10th Report*.
5. SHC, Appendix E 6, Report of the Staffing Sub-Committee, dd 14 September 1904, pp. 1350-2 in Report of the Elementary Committee, pp. 1227-1241, 1240 in *8th Report of the SEC*, 8 November 1904, 1205-414.
6. SHC, op. cit., Appendix E 1, d. 1 February 1905, *10th Report*.
7. SHC, ibid.
8. SHC, *11th Report of the SEC*, 25 July 1905, pp. 931-1162, 941.
9. SHC, *The Surrey Times*, Friday 8 July 1905, 3.

CHAPTER 5
THE STATE OF PT IN SURREY'S ELEMENTARY SCHOOLS – 21 DECEMBER 1905

The SEC noted[1] that the work of Major Norman, who had been appointed on 20 June 1905, was proceeding in respect of classes for teachers where instruction was arranged at Guildford and Sutton and a centre at Wimbledon was being arranged. Two classes were arranged at each centre. The total number attending the classes was 465, of which sixty-five were males.[2]

Since Major Norman was working single-handedly, and, as there was increasing demand for his services, the Committee had requested the Finance and General Purposes Committee to approve the appointment of a qualified assistant to help him. Subsequently, Sergeant Mills was appointed as Assistant Instructor in Physical Training in order to assist Major Norman with his work. His salary was £105 p.a. rising to £110 p.a. after one year's satisfactory service.[3]

Major Norman reported at the end of the Christmas term 1905.[4] Noting that he had inspected 188 schools during the term, he made the following observations on the state of PT in the county:

(1) Teachers
The general standard was insufficiently high. The fault lay with previous drill classes that the teachers had attended which had laid emphasis on their skills as practical exponents rather than instructors. All the teachers impressed Major Norman regarding their appreciation of the value of PT, and, the manner of their attitude was admirable, as the teachers disregarded all personal inconvenience in the interests of the welfare and instruction of their pupils.

(2) Children
Generally, the children presented a healthy appearance and were beneficially fitted to the physical exercises. Nevertheless, there were some exceptions in the poorer districts and the advice of the EMO would be advisable.

(3) System
Of the 188 schools inspected:
147 had adopted the 1904 Syllabus;
32 worked on a combination of the 1904 Syllabus, the Model Course and Military Drill;
9 still adhered to the Model Course.

The reason why there were these discrepancies, appears to be because of a Report of a Physical Training Committee signed by F.H. Burrows, J.C. Colvill and F.H. Trench, Senior Examiner at the Board and the Secretary of the Committee.[5] This Report was unpublished as the Vice-President, Sir John Eldon Gorst (1835-1916) was apparently unwilling to publish it. In the recommendations of this Report the following was stated:

i. That the Model Course of Physical Training appended to the Code by the Board of Education should, after January 1 1903 be made obligatory.
ii. That H.M. Inspectors should be clearly instructed to give their personal aid and encouragement to the formation of classes for teachers under efficient instructors-as was already *being carried out in Surrey and elsewhere by hundreds of teachers who were themselves paying 5/- to 10/- a head besides travelling expenses.* (author's italics) (supra Chapter 2 note 3: *The Surrey Times* 21 June 1902, 6)

It seems clear that Colvill had instituted a series of PT courses based on a presumptive application of the Model Course.

In the schools which had adopted the 1904 Syllabus, the exercises had theoretically been carried out but the desired results had failed to be realised owing to incorrect application which was due to the lack of knowledge by the instructors.

(4) Time Devoted To the Subject
The time devoted to instruction varied from two hours a week to five minutes a day. In some schools part of the time given to training was utilised in swimming, the masters swimming with, and, instructing their pupils with excellent results.

(5) Accommodation
The facilities for imparting instruction in PT varied from the central hall to the overcrowded classroom. There were also few schools in which, with a little imagination, a fairly useful programme of training could not[*sic*] be implemented. However, in a few cases all such training would not be possible in wet weather.

(6) Playgrounds
The playgrounds in respect of PT appeared to be sufficiently good, although they required a lot of improvement to make them suitable as playgrounds. Rain often rendered many of them impossible which meant that they needed re-metalling.

Suggestions for Improvement

(1) All teachers should pass through a class of instruction. Practical work ought not to be imposed compulsorily for teachers physically unfit to take it, but it was desirable that all teachers should have some knowledge of the theoretical elements of the exercises.
(2) The 1904 Syllabus should be uniformly adopted but ought to be introduced gradually as the teachers attending classes of instruction become increasingly qualified to impart instruction.
(3) Time-tables of schools throughout the county should be uniformly implemented and should consist of at least two hours a week. Difficulties might ensue from this suggestion but results might not be what was expected should any less time

be devoted to PT. However, the HMI assured Major Norman that schools which adopted times of between one and a half to two hours a week to the subject compared favourably in educational terms with schools of similar size and conditions.

(4) Swimming should be encouraged wherever possible and any time devoted to it should count as time given to PE.

(5) The formation of school clubs should be encouraged. *PT was not intended to take the place of, but to be supplemental to other games.* Masters tended to extend their tuition to the playing fields in the interests of their own and their pupils' advantage and this ought to be encouraged.

N.B. It is highly unlikely that the Board would have agreed with the statement in italics[6] had it referred to the curriculum proper. It seems to refer to after-school clubs but its context is somewhat ambivalent.

(6) A simple method of recording anthropometrical measurements ought to be instituted in order to record the results of the training in accordance with circular 515.

(7) Inclusion of classes in physical exercises into the curriculum of evening schools should be arranged as far as possible in order to encourage a general interest in the subject and assist a general adoption of the system.

Of the above suggestions, the most important was the necessary provision of efficient instructors so that:

(a) the steps required to be taken for the training of teachers that were presently employed by the SEC were such that they might be able to impart satisfactory training to their pupils in the Elementary Schools, except for those unfit to do so. The classes might consist of:
  (i) a continuous class of daily lessons of not less than two hours a day to last for three weeks or a month
  (ii) a class of one day a week of one hour's duration to last for a period of six months.

Major Norman considered the first option ineffective for its impracticability and so recommended the second option. The aim of the instructor was to impart a general idea of the *Swedish System*, (author's italics), and would not be necessarily exhaustive but its uses and effects, a knowledge of the correct and incorrect methods of actually performing the exercises, and the general qualities required in a drill instructor were the essential elements.

An appeal to teachers should be made through the issue of a certificate of efficiency awarded by the SEC through the Superintendent with a request to the Board to recognise them as an indication of a teacher's competence to teach the 1904 Syllabus.

(b) the means that required to be adopted so that all future teachers on first appointment should be qualified as instructors of PT.

The difficulty of training future teachers in PT was, however, complicated by the fact that of the fifteen Pupil Teacher Centres, only five were under the control of the SEC in respect of PT. Instruction of pupil teachers in those centres out of the control of the SEC were, therefore, restricted to the times when they were working in the elementary schools. Major Norman, therefore, suggested that the Higher Education Committee be approached in order to establish a uniform system of physical training in the secondary schools to which pupil teachers were sent. In that way the SEC would control the training of PT. As far as the five centres were concerned classes of two hours a week should be given. Practical gymnastics should be accompanied by theoretical gymnastics and instruction should also be given in anatomy and physiology.

Suggested Organisation and Staff

Classes for teachers would be organised locally, certain districts being selected in turn with ten or twelve classes running at the same time. Pupil Teacher Centres at Wimbledon, Caterham, Sutton, Woking and Redhill would commence at the same time. As well as a system of instruction, a system of inspection would need to be implemented.

A staff of two instructors in addition to the Superintendent would be necessary with residential access in either Sutton or Guildford. Instructors working from the Pupil Centres of Wimbledon, Caterham and Sutton would be accessible to the former while Redhill and Woking would be available to the latter. Inspection would be undertaken by the instructors where they had instructed.

Major Norman estimated four years as the time necessary for the completion for a full complement of trained PT teachers to be active in the county's schools.

He also estimated a total expenditure of £750 to be spent:

	Salary (£)	**Expenses (£)**
Superintendent	200	100
2 Instructors	200	100
Hire of Halls and Incidental Expenses	75	
Contingencies	75	
Totals	**550**	**200**

Major Norman felt that to employ instructors at £100 was rather a small reward and only ex-soldiers with knowledge of the Swedish system could be employed. However, they lacked the qualities which an instructor should possess to instruct the educated class they would be called on to instruct. The aim, he suggested, should be for SEC to employ appropriate instructors from its own ranks, which instructors would start to become available in approximately four years' time.

The Special Committee (Cognate) recommended acceptance of Major Norman's Report except that which referred to anthropometrical measurements, which, although recommended by circular 515, the Special Committee (Cognate) thought was better to postpone for the time being.[7]

At the end of his report Major Norman had compiled a series of notes on the exercises to be undertaken which the Special Committee (Cognate) agreed to publish.[8]

The Special Committee (Cognate) directed Major Norman to arrange teachers' classes at Woking, Kingston, and, if possible, Farnham.[9]

The Special Committee (Cognate) accepted Major Norman's estimates except for the addition of a further assistant. The estimates were adjusted, therefore, to take account of Sergeant Mill's salary of £105 and the contingencies reduced by £5 to £70 making a total of £650.[10]

Notes

1. SHC, Report of the Elementary Committee, dd 29 September 1905, 20 October 1905, pp. 1528-1542, 1537-1538 in *12th Report of the SEC*, dd 14 November 1905, pp. 1481-1802.
2. SHC, Appendix E.3, Report of the Superintendent of Physical Training, dd 21 December 1905, 333-43 in *13th Report of the SEC*, dd 13 February 1906, pp. 169-449.
3. SHC, Appendix E.1, Report of the Special Committee on Physical Training and Medical Inspection, dd 21 December 1905, pp. 319-20 in op. cit., *13th Report of the SEC*.
4. SHC, op. cit., Appendix E.3, dd 21 December 1905, *13th Report*.
5. TNA, Ed. 24/37A, Report of the Physical Training Committee, Findings of the Committee, 28 October 1901.
6. Ibid., paragraph 3. "That ordinary school games are no substitute for PT even if space were provided for the purpose and that in the comparatively few schools where they obtain, only a small percentage of the children take part in them, while the weakly children are almost necessarily excluded."
7. SHC, op. cit., Appendix E. 1, dd 21 December 1905, *13th Report*.
8. Ibid.
9. Ibid.
10. SHC, Appendix E.1, Report of the Special Committee on PT and MI, dd. 27 March 1906, pp. 796-8 in *15th Report of the SEC*, dd 8 May 1906, pp. 707-882.

CHAPTER 6
CLASSES, CERTIFICATES AND COLONEL FOX

The SEC were favourably disposed to the award of certificates to teachers for PT but the Board did not require any special qualifications in respect of PT. It was, therefore, premature for them to recognise any certificate which gave such a qualification. Nevertheless, the Special Committee on PT and MI approved the suggestion of the Superintendent of PT that, if possible, he should arrange with the Inspector of PT, Colonel Fox, to visit each of the classes and have him authorise, with his signature, an endorsement of the course on the certificate.[1]

The Special Committee on PT and MI had also received an application from the Incorporated British College of PT that the School Teacher's Certificate issued by the College[2] should be recognised as a sufficient qualification for its holder to instruct PT in schools under the authority of the SEC. The Special Committee on PT and MI agreed to recognise this certificate with the caveat that the certificate holder should attend short supplementary classes on the theoretical side of the subject.

At the classes held at Sutton and Guildford 230 teachers obtained certificates of proficiency.[3]

The classes started at Sutton and Guildford on Saturday and Sunday 11 and 12 November were complete.[4] Of those teachers who attended the Sutton classes, 116 were awarded certificates of which ninety-six were awarded to women. At Guildford 109 teachers qualified to receive a certificate of which eighty-two were awarded to women. In addition at a small class of seven at Haslemere, consisting of twenty-five lessons, five received a certificate,[5] totalling 230 in all.

On Monday and Tuesday, 12 and 13 March 1906, Colonel Fox attended the classes at Guildford and Sutton respectively and expressed the opinion of being satisfied at what he saw.

In March 1906[6] there were several classes in motion; two were at Wimbledon terminating in five weeks; two at Kingston; two at Woking and two at Farnham. A further class would start at Dorking on 11 April 1906. When completed, approximately 1,200 teachers were calculated by Major Norman to have completed a course of instruction.[7]

In contemplating the format of the Certificate of Proficiency in PT, the SEC concluded that only PES would be recognised on the certificate itself and was projected in the form shown on the following page[8].

This form was subsequently amended to read on the fifth line, after the word "and", "in the opinion of the Committee".[9]

The Superintendent's next report[10] indicated that he had paid 245 visits to schools. The teachers' class, started at Wimbledon on 25 September 1905, had been completed. Seventy teachers had qualified for a certificate, sixty-one of whom were women. Colonel Fox had endorsed these certificates to the effects that the class had been inspected by him.

The classes that had been completed, at Guildford, Sutton and Wimbledon, therefore, had been attended by 475 teachers and a total of 300 (fifty-six men) had qualified for a certificate.

SURREY EDUCATION COMMITTEE

CERIFICATE OF PROFICIENCY IN PHYSICAL TRAINING

This is to certify that   of
                                        has attended a course of
instruction in Physical Training at
under the direction of the Superintendent of Physical
Training for the County of Surrey, and is competent to give
instruction in this subject in accordance with the Syllabus
of the Board of Education, 1904, in Elementary Schools.

Duration of Course   terminating

Dated the   day of   190 .

.... Chairman of the Committee

.... Secretary

.... Superintendent of Physical
                                                  Training

At the classes he was presently running, 600 teachers were attending, of which 120 were men.[11]

On 8 January 1907, Colonel Fox wrote a letter from the Board to the SEC:

Sir,
I have visited the following Teachers' classes:-

Monday,	12 March 1906,	Sutton
Tuesday,	13 March 1906,	Guildford
Thursday,	10 May 1906,	Wimbledon
Tuesday,	2 October 1906,	Kingston-on-Thames
Monday,	12 November 1906,	Dorking
Wednesday	21 November 1906,	Woking
Friday,	30 November, 1906,	Farnham

The training of the above, consisting of both male and female teachers, was most admirably conducted by Major A Norman, aided by his assistant Sergeant Mills.

The teachers all worked with remarkable earnestness and zeal and performed the exercises with great precision.

I also inspected the following schools and had a good opportunity of seeing the results of the above training. The teachers generally showed an intelligent conception both of the value of PT and of the purposes of each exercise, and handled the classes with confidence.

The children were decidedly more alert and responded with greater promptitude and precision than in old times and it is very evident that they take an interest in their work.

I cannot help adding that I have the greatest admiration for the spirit in which all the teachers I have had the pleasure of meeting, have taken up this form of work and for the intelligent and conscientious way in which they are carrying it out.

Schools Visited: Holy Trinity, Wallington
Burbridge, Godalming
Shalford, Infants
Maybury (Girls) Woking
Maybury (Boys) Woking
Goldsworth, Woking
Singlegate (Girls) Mitcham
Singlegate (Boys) Mitcham
Badshot Lea
Farnham, East Street
Farnham, West Street
Lower Mitcham, Boys
Abbey Road, Infants, Merton

I remain,
Yours faithfully,
(signed) G M Fox

H.M. Inspector of Physical Training[12]

Notes

1. SHC, Appendix E. 1, Report of the Special Committee on PT and MI, dd. 27 March 1906, pp. 796-8 in *15th Report of the SEC*, 8 May 1906, pp. 707-882.
2. McIntosh, Peter C, *Physical Education in England since 1800*, 163-6, 1952, Bell & Hyman, London, Revised and Enlarged Edition 1968.
3. SHC, Appendix E. 2, Report of the Superintendent of PT, dd. 27 March 1906, pp. 799-800 in op. cit., *15th Report of the SEC*.
4. Ibid.
5. Ibid.
6. Ibid.
7. Ibid.
8. SHC, Appendix E. 2, Certificate of Proficiency in PT, in [the first meeting of Medical Inspection and PT Sub-Committee] (MIPTS) [replacing the Special Committee (Cognate)] dd. 27 June 1906, pp. 1248-1252, 1252 in *16th Report of the SEC*, 31 July 1906, 1123-1395.

9. Ibid., 1136.
10. SHC, Appendix E. 3, Report of the Superintendent of PT, dd. 27 June 1906, pp. 1253-4 in op.cit., *16th Report of the SEC*.
11. Ibid.
12. SHC, *18th Report of the SEC*, 12 February 1907, 171-438, 228.

CHAPTER 7
REPORTS OF THE SUPERINTENDENT 1906/1907

In his first report[1] of the 1906/1907 educational year Major Norman noted that Colonel Fox had again inspected the class at Kingston, had expressed approval and endorsed the certificates to the effect that the class had been inspected and passed by him.

He had visited 185 schools. His *raison d'etre* was basically to visit those schools where teachers were being trained.

The army did not adopt the Swedish System, the system upon which the 1904 Syllabus was based, until 1907. According to the Superintendent's report[2], a Danish Army Officer was engaged by the Gymnastic staff at Aldershot to teach Swedish Gymnastics. This officer was Lieutenant Lankilda of the Danish Army. Upon his appointment a radical change took place. Horizontal and parallel bars were replaced by balancing beams and wall bars.[3] Major Norman requested that Sergeant Mills be allowed to undergo a two-monthly course at Aldershot, which he hoped to arrange with the military authorities. The course he had in mind was held in the mornings which would allow Sergeant Mills to fulfil his Surrey duties in the afternoons. Should the SEC agree he requested a sum of £10 from the contingency fund for travelling and other expenses for Sergeant Mills during the attachment.

The Superintendent again noted that swimming would be an obvious alternative to physical exercises in the summer where facilities existed. He requested permission to raise the matter again when he had investigated the subject more, especially in terms of the finance involved. He pointed out that Germany gave a very high value to the physical development of *boys* in German schools and in Denmark all physical training was suspended during the Summer months for swimming to take its place in schools where the appropriate facilities existed.[4]

In his January report,[5] Major Norman noted the completion of courses at Kingston, Woking, Dorking and Farnham, the instruction in the latter two carried out mainly by Sergeant Mills. The first three of these courses consisted of thirty lessons and Farnham's only twenty-five. .The reason for this discrepancy appears to have been that the former three were extended because hot weather in the summer of 1906 made it difficult for teachers to concentrate on the matter in hand. Colonel Fox attended these classes at some point and authorised his usual endorsement of the certificates. These were awarded to ninety male and 265 female teachers in all at these classes.

Altogether, therefore, a total of 643 certificates had been awarded so far.

It was in this report that Major Norman advocated the training of children by the children themselves when the exercises were sufficiently familiar to them. The reason for this seems to have been the size of classes so it made sense to divide the classes into groups, each group having a group leader, who, on the instruction of the teacher would take responsibility for their respective group, thus giving the teacher the opportunity for real supervision. In so doing their confidence, power of command and keenness to learn their duties would be enhanced when they had to carry out the instructions in front of the class as a whole. This system was in force at the Purley National School and its effectiveness was considerable.

The school was not among the most efficient in a PT sense, since none of the teachers had yet attended a course, but the order and regularity (the preparation of the playground, the falling in and marching into school of late comers, the forming up for PT) left little to be desired especially as one of the boys was in direct command. One boy in the class, the Superintendent observed, although very small, had complete control. Major Norman appeared convinced that such a system offered opportunities and a fostering of a readiness for the boys to accept responsibility.

Major Norman was concerned that teachers were apparently too eager to undertake the exercises indoors in cold weather. His solution was that there should be no standing still and the time for each of the exercises accelerated calculating that a total time of ten to fifteen minutes was sufficient.

During the last quarter 162 schools had been visited making a total of 577 since 1 April 1906. There only remained seventeen schools that had not been visited and nineteen that had not been visited by Major Norman himself, which were in districts where it had not been possible to arrange teachers' classes. In the March report Major Norman noted that 190 visits had been made making a total of 767. Classes were started at Richmond and Caterham, the latter not being a convenient centre. The Art room at the County school placed at the disposal of the class was not big enough for the large number of teachers attending. However, at Richmond, the Richmond Drill Hall was hired for the purpose.[6]

In appreciation of the work carried out by Major Norman, in both elementary and secondary schools, the SEC granted a recommendation by the Elementary Committee, supported by the Finance and General Purposes Committee, to raise his salary to £400p.a., of which £300 would be chargeable to the elementary account and £100 to the secondary.[7]

Notes

1. SHC, Appendix E. 3, Report of the Superintendent of Physical Training, dd. 3 January 1907, pp. 323-6 in *18th Report of the SEC*, dd. 12 February 1907, pp.171-438.
2. SHC, Appendix E. 2, Report of the Superintendent of Physical Training, dd. 14 September 1906, pp. 1734-5 in *17th Report of the SEC*, dd. 13 November 1906, 1607-1854.
3. Oldfield, E A L, Lieutenant-Colonel. *History of the Army Physical Training Corps,* 48, Gale & Polden, Aldershot, 1955.
4. SHC, Appendix E.2, op. cit., *17th Report*.
5. SHC, op. cit., Appendix E.3, *18th Report*.
6. SHC, Appendix E. 2, Report of the Superintendent of PT, dd. 24 March 1907, pp. 946-58 in *19th Report of the SEC*, dd. 14 May 1907, pp. 829-1094.
7. Ibid., *19th Report*, 838.

CHAPTER 8
FURTHER REPORTS OF THE SUPERINTENDENT OF PT ON PHYSICAL TRAINING

At the end of the summer term 1907[1] Major Norman referred to the table of exercises at the end of the 1904 Syllabus.[2] These exercises were divided into ten different "groups" with three sections for each of the "groups" considered. They were:-

1. Play, Running or Marching
2. Preliminary Positions and Movements
3. Arm Flexions and Extensions
4. Balance Exercises
5. Shoulder Exercises and Lunges
6. Trunk Forward and Backward Bending
7. Trunk Turning and Sideways Bending
8. Marching
9. Jumping
10. Breathing Exercises

The Syllabus of Physical Exercises for use in Public Elementary Schools, 1905, (1905 Syllabus), which was almost a direct replica of the 1904 Syllabus, had a similar enclosure.

The Superintendent had added his own "Notes on Lectures Given By the Superintendent of Physical Training".[3] His "groups" were six in number, and, instead of a division of three sections, the Superintendent's were divided into four. These were:-

1. Introductory Exercises
2. Arms Bending and Stretching
3. Balance Movements
4. Shoulder Movements
5. Trunk Forward and Backward Bending
6. Trunk Turning and Lateral Bending

As far as the 1904 Syllabus was concerned, he suggested that the table of exercises at the back of the book was only a guide and a suggested set of exercises, not necessarily to be followed in all cases. It was evident, he suggested, that country children who walked considerable distances to and from school required less marching exercises than pupils of the town schools. Nevertheless, country children did not necessarily walk correctly, and needed instruction in marching, more as a lesson than as an exercise. Correct marching meant a saving of energy and a consequent increase in walking endurance.

The time saved in marching exercises might beneficially be applied to the balance exercises in the case of children. The ideal periods of training were twenty minutes per day, with two or three minutes between lessons as "corrective" and "recreative" exercises.[4]

The Superintendent next reported in early September 1907,[5] where he reported visits to have totalled 135 for the last quarter. He again made a plea for children to drill themselves where in some parts of the county he had seen it "admirably done....by little girls of nine". He made mention of "forming up" before entering school as a means by which teachers could establish steadiness "in the ranks".

Classes, suspended during August, were continuing at Richmond, Caterham and Lingfield. In respect of the distances travelled by teachers to attend the courses and with the approach of winter, Major Norman suggested holding the courses on two evenings a week.

Major Norman also made some suggestions regarding new exercises. A "stand easy" was only necessary at the end of each group exercise and not at the conclusion of each exercise. Under ordinary circumstances, a lesson ought to teach each "group" in the table or the chief advantage of the Swedish system, symmetrical development, would not be obtained. The correct order of the groups was shown in the table at the end of the 1904 Syllabus. These groups were, however, by no means compulsory and he again reiterated his opinion that the introductory exercises could be omitted if the pupils had been playing or recently walked to school. Further, a second arm movement could be introduced in the middle of a lesson or take the place of a "trunk turning" or "lateral bending", which had certain physiological effects in common. Nevertheless, unless the instructor was quite satisfied of the advantage to be obtained by such changes, it was better to adhere to the recognised form.

In schools where pupils had undergone the exercises of the 1904 Syllabus for at least two years it was desirable to vary the exercises of the syllabus. They were clearly stated to be examples only and represented a minimum of what was to be done. Teachers should have had no difficulty in thinking out new exercises for their classes but they had to take care to ensure the exercises were of increasing difficulty, which suggests that after a long period of time, not only did the exercises present reducing effort and difficulty but also, perhaps, increasing boredom on the part of pupils.

In very cold weather the Superintendent suggested a formula for a lesson; chaotic running in the playground rather than forming up; an instruction to form up while still running; "number" on the march; open out in a halted position; arm movements; balance; jumping in accordance with the syllabus; marching with arms upward; stretching; quick trunk turning with arms swinging; heels raised with arms upward swinging; double mark time with continuous raised knees and double into school. Major Norman noted that rapid heel raising warmed feet and quick sideways trunk turning with arms sideways stretched warmed fingers.

The important factor was that any new exercises had to be progressive in character with the easy exercises first and the harder ones later. In exercises which emphasised arm positions or movements in combination, the progression of difficulty was hips firm, arms sideways stretched, neck rest, arms forward and arms upwards stretched. Arms forward stretched could be done last with beginners.

Similarly, balance exercises, although there were differences of opinion on the position of the feet in progressive exercises. He suggested; feet closed-attention-astride foot outward, foot forward, foot forward from "feet closed" position, and feet crossed position. To the balance movement there could be added, with the feet in any of the above positions, any arm, or shoulder, or trunk movement, and the movement could become, in an advanced class, a balance, arm or shoulder and trunk movement combined.

In trunk turning, the progression would be: feet closed, attention, followed by the order given above and made more progressive by combining arm movements.

The new exercises would incorporate the following examples and are quoted verbatim:-

Introductions,	any exercises which had been well learned. Leg movement to predominate. Trunk exercises were never to appear as introductory movements.
Arm Exercises,	Right arm upwards, etc., Left arm forward, etc., The above combined with any of the foot positions.
Balance Exercises,	Heels raised in the various foot place positions in the combinations: with head quick turning with arm movements in proper progression or/ with shoulder movements as heels raised with arms upward swinging
Trunk exercises,	Trunk bending, kneeling in arms stretched position
Trunk Turnings,	in the various foot positions with arm movements backward bending in trunk turn position (advanced) and later combined with arm movements Arms flinging with trunk turning swinging with
Lateral Bending,	in the positions of feet closed, etc., etc given above and combined with arm or shoulder movements in their progression
Lunges,	Forward from feet closed position, sideways lunge (the only lunge in which the body must be kept upright) lunging combined with arm and trunk movements, foot backward lunging, etc.,
Jumping,	Long jump and high jump might be included in any PT training

Teachers would have no difficulty in inventing new exercises but had to be careful to avoid cramped chest positions or the holding of breath in a bad combination.

Notes

1. SHC, Appendix E. 3, Report of the Superintendent of PT, pp. 1493-1495 in *20th Report of the SEC*, dd. 30 July 1907, pp. 1343-1536.
2. Board of Education. *Syllabus of Physical Exercises for Use in Public Elementary Schools*, after p.106, HMSO, 1904.
3. SHC, Appendix E. 3, Report of the Superintendent of PT, dd. 21 December 1905, pp. 333-43 in *13th Report of the SEC*, dd. 13 February 1906, pp. 169-449.
4. SHC, Appendix E. 3, pp. 1493-5 in op. cit., *20th Report of the SEC*.
5. SHC, Appendix E. 2, Report of the Superintendent of PT, dd. 7 September 1907, pp. 1972-4 in *21st Report of the SEC*, dd. 12 November 1907, pp.1839-2080.

CHAPTER 9
MORE NOTES ON PT

In the *23rd Report of the SEC*[1] Major Norman indicated that Sergeant Mills had had complete charge of the Redhill and Mortlake teachers' classes, secondary school classes and Evening Continuation classes when, on occasion, *he had been indisposed*. In spite of this 137 schools had been visited during the quarter making a total of 609 for the year. The class at Redhill was attended by twenty-five male and ninety-five female teachers. The total was now 360 men and 1,244 women.

The Superintendent[2] was apparently responsible for Fire Drill and issued a number of instructions since the best preparation for Fire Drill was PT.

Major Norman prepared a further set of notes on PT, Part I, Part II and Part III, for distribution. Part I reiterated the notion of quickness, quietness and order when the class "formed up". To make a lesson in Swedish drill intent on symmetrical training, the easiest exercises of each "group" had to be taught concurrently. There was no need to hurry through the 1904 Syllabus. The crucial point was to teach the elementary positions. So, for example, when a class had been called from the "Stand Easy" position to the "Stand at Ease", the command of "Attention" should never be given until each individual was standing correctly "at Ease". This would clearly take longer with a large class.

The principal requirements in training were: discipline, correctness, vigour and uniformity. Without the first, the others could not be obtained. Twenty minutes was long enough for a lesson as there were ten "groups" to be addressed. In wet weather the lesson ought to be taken at the children's desks for ten minutes.

There were recreative and corrective exercises. Some children had drooping heads and protruding chins, which "head-bending and stretching" could be used encouragingly.

When sitting at a desk the left forearm was not supposed to support the whole weight of the body on the desk. Bending forward should be made at the hips and not in the middle of the back. Shoulders were to be kept square to the front. When sitting up the back should be supported by the back rest where provided. Legs should not be crossed. A book should be read at least twelve inches from the eyes. The chin should be slightly drawn in. A command of Heads Backward Bend now and again was a more effective weapon than advice.

The first essential of good instruction was the art of detecting and correcting mistakes. A good instructor would not walk about putting the children in their places, it was up to them to be in the correct position. The 1904 Syllabus should never be taken *on parade* (author's italics) for reference purposes. Large classes should be divided into sections. In small schools with only one or two teachers the whole school should be given the lesson simultaneously, with the possibility of an efficient older pupil taking the infants.

However, the training of infants was riddled with difficulty since in trying to do their best, a severe nervous strain might develop. The object of training infants was *nutrition*. They should be capable of falling in and opening out on joining the upper school. Lessons for these children should consist mainly of games directed by the teachers. Normal kindergarten games were not rough enough for English boys of six or seven and were not sufficiently *nutritive*.

In cold weather, the Syllabus could be ignored, plenty of running about being required. On departing the classroom, and well warmed after running, the children should fall in on the march, number off on the march, marching with arms up and down, stretching, with heels raising, halt and open out roughly, arm stretchings in succession, deep breathing, lunges, arms flinging or swinging, upward swinging with heels raising, trunk turning quickly with arms sideways stretched, deep breathing, marching with knees raised, doubling with knees raised, halt, open out, foot placings, knee bendings, deep breathing, and march back into school with heels raised.

In summer the spirit and letter of the Syllabus must be adhered to. The heat was unlikely to affect the children when they perspired. Clothing could affect a child as much as the heat so that coats and waistcoats should be removed before exercising. Jumping over a chord would be a satisfactory development of the preliminary jumping exercises.

Part II of the notes was headed Swedish Training. The 1904 Syllabus was essentially representative of a principle, so that one might see a lesson and not recognise a single exercise. The principle was that the *object* of the exercises was consistent with the principles of the Syllabus, which the Syllabus was designed to illustrate. The aim of the Swedish system was to induce quickness – mental and physical, agility, suppleness, symmetrical development, good organic functions, great lung power and endurance. *This might form the Swedish definition of a useful man and they prefer Apollo to Hercules in this respect.*

What Major Norman was distinguishing in this exposition was a contrast with the German system, which was based on a more muscular and apparatus-led philosophy of gymnastics as, for example, the use of the horse and parallel bars.[3]

The Swedish system also claimed other results, mainly educational, discipline, increased will power or concentration, a more intimate connection between the motor centres and the muscles. The exercises of the system were classified into groups and each group designed for a particular purpose. The exercises of each group were further arranged into in order of progressive difficulty. Each exercise was designed to lead up to the one following it. Consequently each preliminary exercise was to be thoroughly mastered before proceeding to the next one.

Major Norman then sought to delineate each of the exercises in turn with explanatory notes on the developmental procedures for the movements of the exercises:-

Introductory Movements and Starting Positions
Arm Exercises
Balance Exercises
Lunges
Shoulder Movements
Backward and Forward Bending
Forward Bending
Lateral Trunk Movements
Marching
Running
Breathing Exercises

Major Norman's exposition of these notes more or less coincided with the tabular groups found at the end of the 1904 Syllabus but were expositions based on his own interpretations.

Part III of the notes was headed "Hints as to Manner of Performing The Exercises" and again Major Norman explained many of the terms used in the explanation of the exercises necessary to the development of Swedish Drill:-[4]

Introductory and Preliminary Movements
Hips Firm
Neck Rest
Heels Raising
Feet Placing
Feet Changing
Arm Movements
Arms Bend
Stretchings

Balance Movements
Knees Bending and Stretching
Leg Raising with Arms Sideways Raise
Leg Raising
Knee Raising
Leg Forward Stretching
Leg Backward Stretching

Shoulder Movements
Forward Raise (Slow Command)
Sideways Raise (Slow Command)
Forward Upwards (Slow Command)
Sideways and Upwards (Slow Commands)
Arms Flinging (Quick Command for Raise)
Arms Forward Bend
Sideways Flinging
Sideways Swinging (Quick "Raise")
Forwards and Sideways Swinging (Quick "Raise")

Lunges
Outward Lunge (A very slow command as in all Lunges)
Forward Lunging

Head and Trunk Exercises
Head Backward Bending
Trunk Backward Bending
Trunk Forward Bend
Arms Flinging
Trunk Bending with Arms Upward Stretched

Turning and Sideways Bending
   Head Turnings and Bendings
   Trunk Turnings
   Arms Swinging
   Sideways Bending
   With Arms Alternate Stretched
   In Sideways Stretch Position

Notes

1. SHC, Appendix M.3, Report of the Superintendent of PT, n.d., pp. 150-74 in *23rd Report of the SEC*, dd. 12 May 1908.
2. SHC, ibid.
3. Puritz, Ludwig, *Code-Book of Gymnastic Exercises*, translated by Knofe, O and McQueen J W, 1-287, Kegan Paul, Trench, Trubner & Co., London. Third Edition, 1905.
4. SHC, op. cit., Appendix M.3, *23rd Report of the SEC*.

CHAPTER 10
THE DEATH OF MAJOR NORMAN

The *24th Report of the SEC*[1] reported that Major Norman was on sick leave owing to a breakdown from overwork. The regret of the SEC encompassed managers and teachers of elementary schools, the report noting that the SEC wished him a speedy and complete recovery. The impact of Major Norman's illness was such that the MIPTS noted that it was unable to submit the usual quarterly report[2] to the SEC. Subsequently, MIPTS reported the death of Major Norman[3] on 19 August 1908. As a result Sergeant Mills[4] took on the duties of Major Norman until his successor Captain Mignon of the Leicestershire Regiment took up the duties of Superintendent of PT on the 17 December 1908.[5]

Major Norman's father was William Frederick Norman born on 27 April 1825. He joined the 2nd Battalion of the 97th Foot on 10 November 1846. He started as an Ensign and became a lieutenant in 1850. He was transferred to the 91st Argyleshire Highland regiment on 20 June 1851. Subsequently he was promoted captain.

Norman's father was married to Diana Truefit on 4 June 1856. There were six children of the marriage: Mary Constance born 1857; William Frederick born 1857; Alice Indiana born 1858; Julia Florence born 1860; Vessey Richard born 1862 and Arthur Ormand born 1865.

Major Norman's birth was registered at Scarborough Registration Office in 1865. He was born in the colonies. He married Katherine Emily Norman (neé Ogston) on 3 October 1894. His wife was born in Aberdeen in 1863. She died on 9 December 1955. She is buried with Major Norman at Haslemere.

The appointment of Major Norman had appeared in the same edition as that of Dr. Thomas Henry Jones, appointed as Education Medical Officer for Surrey, in *The Surrey Times*,[6] which reported on the Surrey Educational Conference that opened on 7 July 1905 at the Surbiton Assembly Rooms. The reporter noted the speech of A W Chapman JP, CA, the chairman of the SEC at the conference, welcoming both Dr. Jones and Major Norman, in which he observed that the appointment of Major Norman was undertaken:

> "in order that the children may have a sound and healthy physical development.....that they may eventually possess strong and active limbs with which to labour...."[7]

That such a conclusion might be reached was determined by the SEC upon the recommendation of the Board to gradually introduce into all schools the 1904 Syllabus and demanded by the 1904 Report. The syllabus to be introduced was to be undertaken by the teachers themselves and not by outside instructors. This was not an attempt – as some people had erroneously imagined – to use the PES as recruiting grounds for the army but rather, as a first priority, to improve the health and physique of the children, and, as a second priority to develop qualities of alertness, decision, concentration and perfect control of mind over body. The Board had indicated that where the exercises portrayed in the 1904 Syllabus could not always be used in the open air, there was a need for the provision of a central hall in large schools and a covered shed in small schools.[8]

Major Arthur Ormand Norman of Inverugie*, Weydown Road, Haslemere, was appointed as Superintendent of Physical Training on 20 June 1905.

He died on 19 August 1908 aged 43 at the home of his sister, Mrs. Norman Layton, who had rented Mr. Allen Chandler's in Bunch Lane, for a term. The funeral took place at 2.30pm at Haslemere Church on 22 August 1908. A full report of the funeral[9] notes the attendance of J C Colvill, who represented the SEC, Colonel and Mrs Malcolm Fox and numerous representatives from the army. His estate at death amounted to £234. 16s. 4d.

The report of his death[10] noted the expeditious and conscientious manner in which he organised the work of developing physical exercises according to the 1904 Syllabus in the elementary schools. However, it did not relate that his duties ranged over not only the 1904 Syllabus in the elementary schools, but also the arrangement of physical exercise in the secondary schools and evening continuation classes. He had also begun the organisation of swimming in the elementary schools. His relations with the teachers of the county were said to be extremely happy and his success in the schools was due to his keenness and he seemed never to know when he had done enough.[11]

A personal eulogy[12] on behalf of Major Norman suggested that he accepted the current concerns of his day that the British race was deteriorating, and as a consequence he dedicated himself to the improvement and physique of the British people. On the completion of his career as a soldier he set out to learn the best system for the fulfilment of this dream. He, therefore, went to Sweden to learn the Swedish System of exercises and when he had mastered it went to Denmark where he perceived that the system of Danish drill was smarter and brighter than the Swedish. There had been an attempt to introduce the army system of drill into the schools with broomsticks instead of rifles, drill sergeants to instruct the teachers, women as well as men. This idea was withdrawn because of the opposition to it, a decision supported by Major Norman for soldiers as well as children since it had no basis in scientific knowledge. In losing his life he found it, for there was no better service to the State than his example of self-sacrifice. Amongst those who have learned of him, it was to be hoped that someone would be found worthy to step into his shoes.

A formal recognition of Major Norman's career[13] was that he was the son of the late Captain W F Norman, Argyll and Sutherland Highlanders. Joining the 3rd Battalion, Royal Fusiliers (Royal Westminster Militia) in January 1884, he was commissioned into the Royal Scots on 25 November 1885 as a Regular Officer. He transferred to the 2nd Battalion, Gordon Highlanders in the same rank (Lieutenant) but with a new date of seniority of 2 January 1886.

At that time, the 2nd Battalion was stationed at Guernsey but by April 1886 he was serving with the 1st Battalion in Malta. In November 1888 Norman moved with the 1st Battalion to Ceylon. Nevertheless, by mid 1890 he had returned to the 2nd Battalion, then stationed in Ireland, including Belfast, Dublin and the Curragh Camp.

He remained with the 2nd Battalion until November 1897, during which period he was stationed at Mayhill Barracks, Glasgow, until September 1896 when the 2nd Battalion moved to Malpaquet Barracks, Aldershot. Promoted to the rank of Captain on 1 February 1896, he was appointed Adjutant of his Battalion. He remained in that post until 17 November 1897 when he went to the 3rd (Buchan) Volunteer Battalion in a similar capacity.

Inverugie (Scottish Gaelic:Inbhir Uigidh) is a small village in Aberdeenshire, Scotland that lies on the entrance to the River Ugie just north of Peterhead

Leaving that appointment in March 1901, he proceeded to South Africa where he served with the 21st Mounted Infantry, as opposed to either of the Regiment's two regular battalions, until February 1902.

Most of the large scale battles were over by this time, a form of guerrilla warfare being carried on by the remaining elements of the Boers.

He was awarded the Queen's South Africa medal with four clasps – Cape Colony, Transvaal, Orange Free State and South Africa 1901.

On his return from South Africa, he took up the duties of adjutant of the Buchan Corps, remaining with it until November 1903. Rejoining the 1st Battalion, the Gordon Highlanders in Glasgow, he was promoted to Major on 9 January 1904, whereupon he moved to the 2nd Battalion stationed in India. Returning on 21 December 1904, he joined the Reserve of Officers, and effectively retired from the army.

Major Norman (back row right).
Photograph courtesy of The Gordon Highlanders Museum

Major Norman (front centre).
Photograph courtesy of The Gordon Highlanders Museum

Major Norman (centre).
Photograph courtesy of The Gordon Highlanders Museum

Major Norman (standing in front of pillar, left).
Photograph courtesy of The Gordon Highlanders Museum

Notes

1. SHC, *24th Report of the SEC*, 28 July 1908, 1126-43, 1139.
2. SHC, Report of the MIPTS, 18 June 1908 in ibid. *24th Report*.
3. SHC, Report of the MIPTS, 1 October 1908, 497 in *25th Report of the SEC*, 10 November 1908.
4. SHC, Appendix M.I., Report of the Assistant Instructor of PT, dd. 30 September 1908, 618-9 in ibid., *25th Report*.
5. SHC, Appendix M.1, Report of the Superintendent of Physical Training, 31 January 1909, 973-5 in *27th Report of the SEC*, 16 March 1909.
6. *The Surrey Times*, 8 July 1905, 3.
7. Ibid.
8. Ibid.
9. Ibid., 29 August 1908, 4.
10. Ibid., 22 August 1908, 4.
11. Ibid.

12. *The Surrey Times*, op. cit., 29 August 1908, 4.
13. *The Army and Navy Gazette*, 29 August 1908, 833.

Other Sources

Canada, British Regimental Registers of Service, 1756-1900.
England and Wales National Probate Calendar
Military Campaign medal and Award Rolls 1793-1949
English Census 1901

CHAPTER 11
THE CONSULTATIVE BOARD AND SERGEANT MILLS

J C Colvill was appointed as chairman of the Special Sub-Committee of the Consultative Board appointed to consider the curriculum of elementary schools at its meeting on 23 May 1906.[1] In its final paragraph[2] it noted that in a well-arranged curriculum, approximately two hours a week should be devoted to PT and that swimming and organised games should be regarded as PT for this purpose. These changes were in accordance with the Codes of Regulations for 1906 and 1907 when organised games and swimming were respectively authorised by the Board.[3]

The Consultative Board suggested that these regulations might be issued to designate that twenty minutes a day or 100 minutes a week should be devoted to the subject.[4] Replies from headteachers[5] concerning the nature and organisation of the curriculum in response to the Consultative's Committee's circular was that they were not in general favourably disposed towards a two-hour-minimum time devoted to PT, since it was difficult to arrange. In some schools, however, the Superintendents' recommendations had been implemented without any difficulty. Some had introduced the twenty-minutes-a-day recommendation.

During the absence of Major Norman, Sergeant Mills was in temporary charge of PT. According to his report, the number of schools visited was, "in the first quarter of the current financial year" seventy with a total for the half year of 154.[6] His report suggested that schools that did not devote twenty minutes a day to the subject were, as a rule, "behindhand". There was also a tendency for instruction to be given indoors in the central hall, instead of outdoors in the open air.

Teachers' classes at Redhill were completed. New classes at Mitcham and Egham had been started on 19 and 24 June 1908. Mitcham had an attendance of 116 (twenty-four men and ninety-two women); Egham seventy, twenty-three men and forty-seven women. Many teachers cycled distances of up to twelve miles to attend the courses.

The numbers from Egham and Mitcham brought the total number of teachers attending classes since their inception was 1876. The number of teachers earning certificates of proficiency at the Redhill and Mortlake classes was seventy-seven and nineteen, respectively, making a total of 953 certificates awarded.[7] At the Horley class, the number of certificates awarded was twenty-six, twenty-two women and four men making the total of certificates awarded 979.[8]

Notes

1. SHC, Appendix E.1, Report of the Special Sub-Committee of the Consultative Board, Appointed to Consider the Curriculum of Elementary Schools, dd. 26 February 1908, pp. 326-45 in *24th Report of the SEC*, dd. 28 July 1908.
2. SHC, ibid., 334.

3. Board of Education, Article 44 (f), Preface, VI, *Code of Regulations for Public Elementary Schools*, HMSO, 1906. And *Code of Regulations for Public Elementary Schools*, 3, 2-9, HMSO, 1907.
4. SHC, op. cit., *24th Report*, 334.
5. SHC, Appendix B, pp. 338-43 in op. cit., Appendix E.1, dd. 26 February 1908, pp. 326-45, op. cit., *24th Report of the SEC*.
6. SHC, Appendix M 1, Report of the Assistant Instructor of PT, 30 September 1908, pp. 618-9 in *25th Report of the SEC*, 10 November 1908.
7. SHC, ibid.
8. SHC, Appendix M.1, Report of the Assistant Instructor of PT, 24 November 1908, pp.740 in *26th Report of the SEC*, 12 January 1909.

CHAPTER 12
THE APPOINTMENT OF CAPTAIN MIGNON AS SUPERINTENDENT OF PT

In response to the vacancy of Superintendent of PT on the death of Major Norman, the SEC received thirty-six applications.[1] Two candidates were chosen for the final selection, Captain John Murray, late of the Black Watch and Captain J. E. Mignon, late of the Leicestershire Regiment.

Captain Mignon took up his duties on 16 December 1908. He had taken the opportunity of consulting the Assistant Instructor to assess the current state of affairs. Additionally, he had visited eighteen schools, Teachers' classes and Evening Continuation Schools.

The number of visits since Sergeant Mills's last report on 24 November 1908 was seventy-nine, making a total of 339 since the beginning of the last financial year, the figure in the last report being wrongly quoted, which should have been 260. Captain Mignon was pleased with the state of things as he had seen them; discipline, physical drill and Fire Drill. The latter had been imposed by the code of 1907 along with swimming. Insufficient time had been allocated to PT but a standard of twenty minutes a day was *henceforth* to be adopted. Presumably, this standard had been part of his negotiation upon his appointment.

He was intent on creating a spirit of emulation amongst the pupils. He had, in the schools visited so far, suggested to teachers that classes should be divided into three sections. The first section was to consist of those pupils best at drill, the second, those that were fair and thirdly those who are the worst. When falling in, the first section should be on the right, the second in the centre and the third on the left. Apart from creating a spirit of emulation, a spirit of rivalry would also be engendered. Any pupil insufficiently good to be in section three would receive individual tuition until capable of being drafted into section three.

Captain Mignon also wished to present displays at certain centres, where invited teachers could observe the work of other schools. In this way teachers would learn what others were doing in their own county *with the same material as that which they themselves had*.

The decision to allow student and pupil teachers to qualify for certificates in PT was very welcome since they gave instruction in schools.

Colonel Fox inspected the Egham teachers' class on 16 December 1908 and the Mitcham class on 22 December. One hundred and twenty-two teachers attended the Mitcham class, twenty-three men and ninety-nine women, of whom fifty-seven passed for certificates, twelve men and forty-five women. At Egham, the attendance was seventy-six, twenty-four men and fifty-two women, of whom forty passed, thirteen men and twenty-seven women receiving certificates. The total number of certificates awarded so far was, therefore, 1,087.[2]

Notes

1. SHC, Report of the Finance and General Purposes Committee, 13 November 1908, 11 December 1908 in *26th Report of the SEC*, dd. 12 January 1909, 698.
2. SHC, Appendix M.1, Report of the Superintendent of PT, 31 January 1909, pp. 973-5 in *27th Report of the SEC*, dd. 16 March 1909.

CHAPTER 13
ESTIMATES FOR 1909/1910

The estimates for PT for 1909/1910 were £290 less than the year previously:-

	£
Salary of Superintendent	250.00
Salary of Assistant Instructor	135.00
Travelling Allowance of: Superintendent	100.00
Asst/Instructor	60.00
Instruction in Swimming	130.00
Special printing and contingencies	35.00
	710.00[1]

The Superintendent noted the start of four more teachers' classes at Epsom on 22 March 1909 with an attendance of 140. The hall was suitable, however, for only eighty people at the most, which meant that two classes were formed out of the total number. A course began at Guildford on 23 March 1909 with a total number of 203 people. A course at Camberley was started on 25 March 1909 with an attendance of sixty-three.[2]

These classes were subsequently inspected by Colonel Fox and his findings reported to the MIPTS,[3] which expressed their appreciation of the assistance he had given by his inspection of the classes. Subsequently, MIPTS referred the terms of Captain Mignon's appointment to the Finance and General Purposes Committee, since, in the first instance, his original appointment had been for one year from 16 December 1908.

As a result of the MIPTS report and the subsequent referral to the Elementary Committee, Captain Mignon's salary was raised to £350 p.a. as from 16 December 1909 to rise by yearly incremental amounts of £25, to a maximum of £400.[4] Captain Mignon also withdrew his suggestion that there could be demonstration classes of this or that school to another because of "practical difficulties" leaving open the possibility of head teachers visiting schools within their vicinity to assess the work being done there.[5]

Captain Mignon's report[6] of November 1909, stated that 592 schools had been visited in the "current financial year". Five teachers' classes had just been terminated. Two, undertaken at Guildford, terminated on 2 November 1909, with an attendance of 228, fifty-four men and 174 women. A previous report had suggested that the numbers involved were 208 indicating that teachers could join within a certain time of the course starting. With an attendance of 228, it is not surprising that the Superintendent split them into two classes. Of the 228, twenty-eight – six men and twenty-two women – had previously been awarded certificates. Of the remaining 200, 109 were awarded certificates – twenty-nine men and eighty women.

At Epsom, the two classes ended on 8 November 1909. One hundred and sixty teachers, forty men and 120 women, attended. Of these twenty-eight already held County certificates, one man and twenty-seven women. Of the remaining 132, eighty-six were awarded certificates – thirty-two men and fifty-four women.

At Camberley, the course closed on 11 November 1909. Eighty teachers attended, twenty men and sixty women. Of these, four women already held County certificates. Of the remaining seventy-six, forty-eight had received certificates – ten men and thirty-eight women.

Colonel Fox had inspected on 12, 11 and 14 October, respectively (i.e. Guildford, Epsom and Camberley), and authorised the *usual endorsement to be made on the certificates.**

Arrangements had been made at Kingston for seven classes to begin at the Y.M.C.A. Gymnasium, Kingston owing to the large number of applications received. The first class started on 18 November 1909, each of the classes comprising about forty-four teachers.

Captain Mignon requested that teachers who held certificates but desired to attend a second course should have their original certificates endorsed to that effect, which would be an act of justice as otherwise they would have nothing to show for their attendance at a second course. He also noted that he had examined most of the teachers who had recently attended classes, mainly infant teachers, in the practical work in their schools, since they were better able to do themselves justice when taking their own classes of children.[7]

* Note: *see* Appendix XIII for a complete analysis of courses and inspections made by Colonel Fox.

Notes

1. SHC, Report of the MIPTS, dd. 1 April 1909, 59-65, 60 in *28th Report of the SEC*, 11 May 1909.
2. SHC, Appendix M.1, Report of the Superintendent of PT, dd. 26 March 1909, pp.101-3 in ibid., *28th Report of the SEC*.
3. SHC, Report of the MIPTS, dd. 25 November 1909, pp. 762 in *31st Report of the SEC*, dd. 11 January 1910.
4. SHC, ibid., *31st Report*.
5. SHC, Appendix M.1, Report of the Superintendent of PT, dd. 26 March 1909, pp.101-3 in op. cit., *28th Report*.
6. SHC, Appendix M.1, Report of the Superintendent of PT, dd. 21 November 1909, pp. 827-9 in op. cit., *31st Report*.
7. Ibid.

CHAPTER 14
MILITARY DRILL AND THE SEC

The period 1870-1914 was notable for the lobby in favour of endeavouring to secure military drill within the curriculum of the PES.[1] One aspect of those in favour of military drill's introduction into the PES curriculum was its disciplinary character.[2] In this respect, it had its uses:

> "*Military drill* alone is insufficient as a means of physical culture, and should only be used as a supplementary measure in the physical education of children. Its use fails to bring the chest, shoulders, and arms into vigorous action............muscular action ...almost totally confined to the lower limbs. Still it has its uses for it is strictly essential in the preliminary positions which precede the introduction of physical exercises."[3]

Seaborne and Lowe quote the 1902/3 Board of Education Report to the effect that military drill was systematically taught to PES boys in 6,437 day schools.[4]

Nevertheless, there was a growing call for military drill other than that of a disciplinary measure. In January 1902, *The Times*[5] published a letter from Sir Thomas Lauder Brunton (*see* Appendix XI for biographical details), founder of the National League for Physical Education and Improvement in 1905,[6] suggesting that:

> ".....let all children be taught at school, partly in play and partly as work how to handle a gun, how to shoot and how to manoeuvre "[7]

Brunton's letter was a response to a poem, *The Islanders*, printed in *The Times*[8] a few days earlier that was critical of the games ethic of the time, which characterised the state of the nation as more interested in cricket and football:

> "with the flannelled fools at the wicket or the muddied oafs at the goals "[9]

What was required was a development of those childish games *I Spy, French and English* and *Prisoners Base* adapted to the needs of modern warfare. In this way, boys aged fourteen would be sufficiently trained to defend the country in case of invasion. Should there be an invasion, there would be a sufficiently trained army to defend the country without the need for recourse to conscription.[10]

In the late 19th century and early 20th century, however, the thrust of Britains's defences were mainly concentrated on the navy. The navy had always been at the heart of Britain's national interest. The "Blue Water School" in England was typical of an imperialist grouping devoted to naval technology that was apparent across Europe.[11]

Navies had always had a primary importance in the creation and maintenance of empires. In the age of imperialism naval strength was an almost ideological condition of defence policy. "New Navalism" dominated a large-scale expansion of naval war potential as the central aggression among the great world powers.[12]

The foundation of the German Reich in 1871 had made a deep impression on the world. Public opinion in Britain suggested that, Bismarck's brilliance apart, Germany's rise was attributed primarily to its military efficiency. Inferences were drawn from this about the importance of the military in the creation, expansion and maintenance of world powers.[13]

Kaiser Wilhelm II admired and envied Britain's position, which clearly depended above all on her strength at sea. The misfortunes of Germany's history had thwarted her right to be a great colonial empire and the world power status, which he felt Germany deserved. It was, therefore, essential to build a great navy in opposition to Britain.

Wilhelm's ambitions in this direction were influenced by the Admiral von Senden-Bibran, the head of his naval cabinet and Admiral Tirpitz, head of the central naval agencies, who worked fruitfully with the Flottenverein Naval Association, in order to win over public opinion in Germany. In 1897 Tirpitz became minister of marine and the Navy League was founded in 1898. The Kaiser was also influenced by a book by the American Admiral Mahon who wrote *The Influence of Sea Power upon History, 1890*, which the Kaiser subsequently ordered, in translation, to be placed in every ship in the German navy.[14]

During the 1890s Germany accelerated her colonial policies and increased pressure on Britain's worldwide interests, a policy known as *Weltpolitik*. After challenging British interests in Samoa and the Congo, in 1896 the Kaiser sent a provocative telegram to President Kruger congratulating the Boers on having dealt with the threat of the Jameson raid, in itself a serious embarrassment to Britain. Meanwhile Germany was extending her interests in the Balkans and the Middle East with the aim of building a rail link between Berlin and Baghdad.[15] All in all, the Kaiser summed up his naval policy:

> "I will never rest until I have raised my Navy to a position similar to that occupied by my Army. German colonial aims can only be gained when Germany has become master of the ocean."[16]

The significance of this policy for the naval powers of Britain and Germany was that it played a crucial part in the alienation of the two countries. In Britain the navy had always known national status because of its critical role at the heart of Britain's national interest. In Germany it had first to be *made* popular. This was successful because of Kaiser Wilhelm II and Admiral Tirpitz. Nevertheless, there were those who perceived that the long-term impact of the naval policies of Britain and Germany had possible dangerous consequences:

> "Here is the first great racial struggle of the future; here are two great nations pressing against each other, man to man, all over the world. One or other has to go; one or other will go."[17]

Ideological inferences surrounded the notions of empire and militarism. Imperialism was, as it were, a derogatory term which didn't enter the vocabulary of political debate. Militarism, however, was particularly associated with Germany, which had a conscripted army and which was said to be Germany's greatest strength.[18]

In 1906, though, the SEC had the opportunity to confound a military construct in the elementary schools. A resolution from Quarter Sessions was received with particular reference to the introduction of military training in schools.[19] At the Court of Quarter Sessions held on Tuesday 2 January 1906 at the County Hall, Kingston-on-Thames, it was resolved:

> "that a Committee be appointed to consider the question of giving instruction in military drill and the use of the rifle in all schools receiving grants from the

Public Funds, and of encouraging rifle clubs and rifle shooting in the County, and to report thereon."[20]

Subsequently, the SEC reported that they had received several applications for permission to include rifle shooting for boys in the upper departments of some elementary schools, which they referred to the Committee appointed to consider the question.[21]

The Joint Committee decided that the enquiry resolved itself into two elements:
(a) The provision of instruction in Military Drill and the use of the rifle in all schools receiving grants from the Public Funds
(b) The encouragement of rifle clubs and rifle shooting in the County.[22]

In effect, the two elements related to those questions, which in (a)[23] referred to schools, whereas (b)[24] was not within the competence of the SEC.

As far as (a) was concerned the enquiry noted that the number of boys in elementary schools and institutions in Surrey was 40,946, of which 8,607 were aged between twelve and fifteen. Seventeen were over the age of fifteen.

The contemporary situation was that Major Norman had arranged for physical exercises on the basis of the 1904 Syllabus to be taken in the open air where practicable.

In at least three of the PES, instruction was given to older boys in rifle shooting, the expenses of which were paid for by voluntary effort. Enquiries to other counties revealed that none had introduced Military Drill in elementary schools at the expense of public funds.

The Board, in a letter dated 18 May 1906 had expressed themselves:-

"The Board of Education would be prepared to consider proposals for the inclusion under Article 44(a) of the Code of a scheme for teaching Rifle Shooting in the curriculum of a Public Elementary School upon the following conditions:

(a) Special care should be taken that the time allotted to the proposed instruction shall not unduly encroach upon the time at present required for PT. The Board regard careful attention to an all round system of physical development as an essential preliminary and accompaniment to any special exercises as rifle shooting;

(b) Rifle shooting should be restricted to boys of proper physique and to boys who have reached the age of 12;

(c) A short definite scheme of instruction should be submitted."

However, the result of the Committee's enquiry was that the Committee did not consider it expedient that instruction in military drill and rifle shooting should be recognised as a subject in the curriculum of PES maintained out of public funds. The reason was that in the opinion of the Committee the existing 1904 Syllabus of instruction in PT was better suited to the age and physical capacity of elementary school children and well adapted to cultivate a proper tone of discipline and alertness to prepare them for more advanced instruction.

Nevertheless, in view of the Board's letter of 18 May 1906, the Committee was disposed to approve the introduction in special cases of instruction in rifle shooting in PES and the continuance of such instruction where it was already in instruction. However, the instruction had to be given under an organised system and under proper supervision to boys over twelve and that the system introduced was established and maintained by voluntary effort.

The Committee considered that instruction in drill and rifle shooting a proper subject for recognition in the curriculum of Evening Continuation Schools and also in secondary schools. Governors in secondary schools should be encouraged to establish Cadet Corps in such schools. Any scheme that promoted proposals within this paragraph were deserving of encouragement and financial support out of public funds.

The enquiry was signed off by A W Chapman, Chairman of the Committee and the SEC on 6 October 1906.

Nevertheless, concerns of German invasion grew. The threat of a German naval expansion was crucial to these concerns. From June 1897 Admiral Tirpitz, minister of marine until the outbreak of hostilities in 1914, supported almost unconditionally by Wilhelm II had initiated the idea of creating a German navy that would challenge the British position on the high seas. In 1898 a plan was borne that outlined the building of twelve new battleships, ten new large cruisers and twenty-three new small cruisers within six years to add to its existing navy of two and seven vessels, which it already had in these respective categories.[25]

On top of that Germany began to woo Turkey in respect of opening up rail networks as far as Basra in order to thwart Russian expansion. Further her population began a rapid expansion. An opportunity also arose for Germany to gain a foothold in China cemented by treaty, which created a scramble for western powers to gain territory there as well.[26]

"This is the State above the Law
The State exists for the State alone"[27]

Notes

1. Penn, Alan, *Targeting Schools*, 160, Woburn Press, London, 1999.
2. McIntosh, Peter C., *Physical Education in England since 1800*, 109, Revised and Enlarged Edition, Bell and Hyman, 1968.
3. Chesterton, Thomas, *The Theory of Physical Education in Elementary Schools*, 23, Gale and Polden Ltd., London, 1895.
4. Seaborne, Malcolm and Lowe, Roy, *The English School; its architecture and organization, Volume II 1870-1970*, 69, Routledge & Kegan Paul, London, 1977.
5. *The Times*, 7 January 1902, 10
6. Penn, Alan, op. cit., 123-4
7. *The Times*, op. cit., 7 January 1902.
8. Ibid., 4 January 1902, 9.
9. Kipling, Rudyard, *The Complete Verse*, 240-1, 1990, Kyle Cathie Edition, London, 2006.
10. *The Times*, op. cit., 7 January 1902, 10.
11. Gollwitzer, Heinz, *Europe in the Age of Imperialism 1880-1914*, 96, Thames & Hudson, London, 1969.
12. Ibid.
13. Ibid., 94-5.
14. Anderson, M S, *The Ascendancy of Europe 1815-1914*, 341, 1972, Pearson Education Limited, Edinburgh, 3rd Edition 2003.
15. Lee, Stephen J, *Imperial Germany 1871-1918*, 72, Routledge, London, 1999.
16. Marriott, J A R, Sir, *A History of Europe from 1815 to 1939*, 403, 1948, Methuen & Co., 5th Edition.
17. Anderson, M S, op. cit., 342.

18. Penn, Alan, op. cit., 165.
19. SHC, Report of the Elementary Committee, dd. 15 December 1905 and 10 January 1906, pp.211-222 in *13th Report of the SEC*, dd. 13 February 1906, 169-449.
20. Ibid.
21. SHC, Report of the Elementary Committee, pp. 1654-1663, in *17th Report of the SEC*, dd. 13 November 1906, 1607-1854.
22. SHC, Report of the Joint Committee as to Military Drill & Rifle Shooting, dd. 18 October 1906, pp. 1855-9, Appointed pursuant to Resolutions of Quarter Sessions dd. 2 January 1906 and the County Council dd. 13 February 1906 in *Surrey Quarter Sessions and SCC*, dd. 13 November 1906, pp.1855-74.
23. SHC, Appendix A, dd. 6 October 1906, 1860-74 in ibid., *Surrey Quarter Sessions and SCC*, dd. 13 November 1906.
24. SHC, Appendix B, in ibid., *Surrey Quarter Sessions and SCC*, dd. 13 November 1906.
25. Thomson, David, *Europe Since Napoleon*, 534, first published in Longmans 1957, Penguin Books, Harmondsworth, Middlesex, 1966.
26. Ensor, R C K, *England 1870-1914*, 258-9, The Clarendon Press, Oxford, 1936.
27. Kipling, Rudyard, 'A Death-bed', 109, in Gardner, Brian, *An Anthology, Up The Line To Death, The War Poets 1914-1918*, Methuen, 2007.

CHAPTER 15
THE PERSISTENCE OF THE MILITARY DRILL LOBBY AND THE REVISED 1909 SYLLABUS

The persistence of the military drill lobby was a pervasive thorn in the side of those who did not believe it was a necessary concomitant to a defence of the realm. A National Service (Training and Home Defence) Bill, which had been introduced into the Lords on 19 May 1909, was not followed up.[1] Various other attempts were subsequently made but institutions, such as the Trades Union Congress (TUC), were vehemently and emphatically opposed.[2]

In the debate on the first Bill in the House of Lords Lord Meath displayed his usual mind-set on the topic:

> "What we want is discipline.....in the upper classes.....in the middle classes......and in the lower classes.......If there were more discipline there would not be so many slackers who thought nothing of the State or the community and whose sole idea was pleasure, pleasure, pleasure. These notions were not observable in Germany. What confronts this country is the moral danger, the slackness and the indiscipline. What was required was a public opinion favourable to military training."[3]

It seems clear that this was far from the minds of the educational administrators at the Board. In July 1909 Lewis Amherst Selby-Bigge (1860-1951) and the then Chief Inspector of HMI for elementary schools, Edmond Gore Alexander Holmes (1850-1936) jointly issued a memorandum[4] concerning the teaching of dancing in elementary schools raised by Staincliffe C of E School in Batley.

Essentially, dancing was seen to considerably improve the carriage of the children. It made them less clumsy and more supple and trained the children to move quickly, neatly, rhythmically and gracefully. The alertness, precision and self-control required were valuable qualities and even though aesthetic appreciation might not enter the psyche of either teachers or scholars the re-creative character of the exercises was an incentive to stimulate interest in physically exercises generally. Inspectors, however, should take care to ensure that:

(a) dancing should not replace the time devoted to other subjects or take the place of systematic PT
(b) teachers had to be proficient and be able to make lessons profitable for children
(c) a syllabus of dances should be submitted and approved
(d) dancing exercises should be progressively arranged in both an educational and re-creative manner
(e) in mixed schools careful consideration ought to be given to the desirability of boys and girls dancing together.[5]

Morris dances, Old English country dances, the jig, reel, Welsh dance and so on were more desirable since they had attributes that were not found in the minuet, gavotte, pavane and ballroom dances. The peasant dances, by which was meant the former type of dances, were imbued with the spirit of the people, active and vigorous in movement and were able to be performed by men, women, boys and girls with little, if any, personal contact and were also intended for the open air. These dances could also be danced on a playground surface.

The Board were to incorporate these ideas into T*he Syllabus of Physical Exercises for Public Elementary Schools 1909* (1909 Syllabus), which purported to be a revision of the 1905 Syllabus. In fact, although the essence of the 1909 Syllabus remained substantially based on the Swedish Drill system there were some considerable differences in the presentational format of the syllabus.

These were set out as:-

1. a prefatory memorandum consisting of 4 pages
2. Chapter I consisting of an introduction of 20 pages
3. Chapter II   General Directions to Teachers - 5 pages
4. Chapter III   Description of Simple Exercises and Positions - 24 pages
5. Chapter IV   Marching, Running, Jumping, and Breathing Exercises - 9 pages
6. Chapter V   The Arrangements of the Class - 5 pages
7. Chapter VI   Order and Progression of Exercises - 7 pages
8. Chapter VII Tables of Exercises with Introduction - 3 pages
    Series A (for children 7-9 years) - 25 pages
    Series B ("   "   9-11 "   ) - 25 pages
    Series C ("   "   11-14 ") - 25 pages

The chapters thus closed on page 148 but were followed by five appendices:-

A. Supplementary Physical Exercises:-
   (a) Abdominal Exercises   3 pages
   (b) Skipping Exercises   1 page
   (c) Dancing Steps   3 pages
   (d) Games   5 pages
B. Class Room Exercises   1 page
C. Physical Exercises for Infants   3 pages
D. A Suitable Dress for Girls   1 page
E. Suggestions on the Construction of Tables of Exercises   4 pages

There is a total of 168 pages altogether, which differed substantially from both the 1904 and 1905 Syllabuses, both of which had 106 pages with tables at the end. The arrangement of the 1905 Syllabus was:

a preface   - 5 pages
an introduction   - 16 pages
with the Syllabus basically addressing itself to the exercises themselves as:
Syllabus of Exercises:
   Preliminary – Class Arrangements   - 9 pages
   Elementary Starting Positions   - 5 pages
   Arm Flexions and Extensions   - 5 pages

Balance Exercises	- 6 pages
Shoulder Exercises	- 5 pages
Lunge Exercises	- 6 pages
Head and Trunk Exercises.	
Forward and Backward Bending	- 6 pages
Turning and Sideways Bending	- 6 pages
Marching	- 8 pages
Jumping	- 4 pages
Deep Breathing Exercises	- 4 pages
Illustrations	- 15 pages
Specimens of Supplementary Exercises for Children over 12	- 1 page
Appendix (Key Table)	- 2 pages

The 1909 Syllabus was therefore an expansionist philosophy on the notions of what PE actually was. Swedish drill remained in the ascendancy but the battlements, while they had been breeched, were to remain the predominant feature of the PES PE curriculum until the beginning of the Second World War and beyond. However, in one sense the 1909 Syllabus put to bed the question of military drill in the PES although there were pockets of approval for a voluntary approach to the conceptual acceptance of military drill in certain circumstances.

In September 1909 *Circular 727*[6] was issued by the Board drawing attention to the Revised Syllabus of Physical Exercises for PES. Paragraph 5 of *Circular 727* considered that the Revised Syllabus should be adopted in all PES as soon as possible. The development of children's physique was of national importance.[7] The Syllabus was not an effective remedy for all defects that affected children in the PES but the principles on which the Syllabus was based were sound. The Leas were, therefore, called upon to implement a system, which the Board believed would promote the moral, mental and physical development of the children in the PES and to ensure that each child received a training that would fit him/her to perform the duties of life with vigour and success. It is, perhaps, significant that Lieutenant-Commander (later Captain F H Grenfell, DSO – Appendix XIV) had been appointed to the Board as HMI for Physical Training in 1909, and was subsequently to succeed Colonel Fox.

In September 1909, the 1909 Syllabus was considered by the MIPTS. MIPTS considered the Syllabus to be a revised edition of the 1905 Syllabus with certain additions and alterations. Careful consideration regarding implementation of the Syllabus, was required and a sub-committee appointed to consider and report.

Subsequently, MIPTS met[8] and considered the report of the sub-committee appointed to consider the question of the 1909 Syllabus. Their recommendations included the following:-

1. the attention of the Board be called upon the desirability of the Board to annotate the tables in the 1909 Syllabus with references given to the words of command in earlier tables;
2. that changes introduced in the new Syllabus be incorporated gradually into the system of PT at present in force, except for the words of command and execution of the exercises, and also subject to those notifications which might be suggested by the Superintendent of PT from time to time and authorised by the Committee;
3. Copies of the 1909 Syllabus be issued to schools as required for the purpose of the Introductory Chapters, I and II, Chapter VI and the Tables of Exercises, the latter to be adopted as the basis for schemes of instruction;

4. the Memorandum of the Superintendent attached to the report[9] be issued with the new Syllabus.

The SEC approved[10] the course of action taken by MIPTS.

The memorandum of the Superintendent was dated 27 January 1910.[11] It contained the recommendations approved of by the MIPTS above. However, Chapters III and IV containing additional exercises and some changes in the words of command should be adopted. The words of command found in the 1905 Syllabus should be adhered to with the following exception: "Arms across – bend" to replace "Forward Bend in Arms Flinging" (p.45 of the 1909 Syllabus).

There were only two cases where an alteration in method of execution of the exercises should be made:-
1. standing at ease where the arms behind the back should be fully extended to ensure expansion of the chest.
2. in the arms bend position, the whole of the upper arm should be close to the body and the finger tips touching the shoulder (figure 37)

Order and Progression of Exercises

Chapter VI should be carefully studied and the progression of exercises listed at the top of page 65 implemented.

Additional Exercises

All additional exercises appearing in the 1909 Syllabus should be adopted. The seventeen new exercises in Chapters III and IV, for example, head bending forward (p.29) and a few in the Tables of Exercises on pages 74-148 should also be implemented, the Scheme of these exercises were set forth on page 71.

Appendices

Appendices A, B and C should also be studied.

Note: *See* Appendix XV for an advert on Rifle Practice for Elementary Schools published in *The Schoolmaster*, 17 February 1912.

Notes

1. Penn, Alan, *Targeting Schools*, 147-8, Woburn Press, London, 1999.
2. *The Times*, 8 September 1909, 4
3. *Hansard*, House of Lords, National Service (Training and Home Defence) Bill, 12 July 1909, column 329.
4. TNA Ed. 22/9, Board of Education, The Teaching of Dancing Steps and Exercises to Scholars in Public Elementary Schools, Memo to Inspectors, E. No. 39, 24 July 1909, pp. 1-2.
5. Ibid.
6. Board of Education, *Circular 727*, No Title, dd September 1909; *see also* McIntosh, Peter C, *Physical Education in England since 1800*, 156-60, Bell and Hyman, London, 1968.
7. Board of Education, op. cit., *Circular 727*.
8. SHC, Report of the MIPTS, 3 February 1910, 894 in *32nd Report of the SEC*, 15 March 1910.
9. SHC, Appendix M.1, Memorandum To Accompany The Syllabus of Physical Training (1909), dd. 27 January 1910, pp. 1060-1in ibid., *32nd Report*.
10. SHC, *32nd Report of the SEC*, dd. 15 March 1910.
11. SHC, op. cit., Appendix M.1, dd. 27 January 1910, *32nd Report*.

CHAPTER 16
REFORMED SUB-COMMITTEES

The *33rd Report of the SEC* noted the demise of MIPTS, its work being re-constructed into two separate functions:
(a) the MI Sub-committee for the medical work
(b) the PT element of the work was transferred to the School Management Sub-Committee.[1]

The work of the School Management sub-committee was to deal with special subjects, staffing, stock and stores, all questions relating to the curriculum, the proper organization and classification of the scholars and the reports of the Inspection of the Board of Education and the Committee.[2]

In his report of 22 March 1910[3] the Superintendent noted that 157 schools had been visited making a total of 860 in the current financial year. The new syllabus had to be explained. Additionally, Colonel Fox had inspected seven classes at Kingston on 8, 10 and 14 March recommending the usual endorsement on certificates on the termination of the course.[4]

The cost of PT for the year 1910/1911 was estimated at £850 for the year:

	£
Superintendent's salary	358.00
Assistant Instructor's salary	140.00
Travelling allowance of the Superintendent	100.00
Travelling and out-of-pocket expenses of the asistant instructor	75.00
Instruction in Swimming	150.00
Contingencies	27.00
	850.00[5]

The average cost for the year 1908/1909 MI and PT on the Elementary Education Account was £2,762. 11s. 7d.

The next report of the Superintendent noted that 197 schools had been visited since the last visit. Difficulties arose with the 1909 Syllabus so he proposed one session classes at various central halls at available schools during the Autumn term so that no expense would be incurred by the SEC.[6] Subsequently approved, with J C Colvill appointed as chairman of the School Management Committee, the Sub-committee also requested that all schools visited by the Superintendent were to be reported to it by him.[7]

In the next report,[8] the Superintendent noted that he had visited 214 schools, although the detailed list for the elementary schools totalled 174:-

Wimbledon	1	Mitcham	9	Merton	3
Barnes and Mortlake	7	Richmond	4	Egham	3
Godstone	12	Kingston	4	Camberley and Bagshot	6
Oxted	4	Surbiton	4	Woking	11
Caterham	6	Esher and Dittons	3	Guildford	19
Purley, Coulsden Kenley	9	Godalming	3	Oxshott	1
Haslemere	3	Sutton	6	Weybridge	2
Dorking	19	Chobham	3	Wallington	3
Horley	8	Carshalton	3	Effingham	3
Walton on Thames	1	Lingfield	3	Malden	1
Chertsey	4	Morden	1	Cobham	2
Banstead	3				

Notes

1. SHC, *33rd Report of the SEC*, dd. 10 May 1910, pp. 1-214, 7.
2. SHC, Report of the Elementary Committee, dd. 8 April 1910, pp. 44-54, in ibid., *33rd Report*.
3. SHC, Appendix M.1, Report of the Superintendent of PT, dd. 22 March 1910, pp. 117-21 in ibid., *33rd Report*.
4. Ibid.
5. SHC, Report of the MIPTS, dd. 31 March 1910, 65 in ibid., *33rd Report*.
6. SHC, Schedule B, Report of the Superintendent of PT, pp. 372 in Appendix E. 4, Report of the School Management Sub-Committee, 3 and 24 May 1910 and 14 June 1910, pp. 360-73 in *34th Report of the SEC*, dd. 26 July 1910, pp. 215-460.
7. SHC, Appendix E. 4, Report of the School Management Sub-Committee, dd. 14 June 1910, pp. 360-73 in ibid, *34th Report*.
8. SHC, Schedule B, Report of the Superintendent of PT, pp. 578-9 in Appendix E. 3, Report of the School Management Sub-Committee, 28 June 1910, 13 July 1910 and 27 September 1910, p. 567 in *35th Report of the SEC*, 8 November 1910, pp. 461-664.

CHAPTER 17
1910 TO AUGUST 1914

The 360 attendances at the Kingston 6 course meant that, during 1910, 1,763 teachers had received instruction in the 1909 Syllabus of Physical Exercises.[1]

The Superintendent was keen to recommend that twenty minutes in the morning session of each day was spent on PT for all departments other than infants for whom he favoured fifteen minutes. His rationale for a twenty-minute-a-day lesson was that the tables of exercises in the 1909 Syllabus were based on a length of twenty minutes. He also commented on the School Dress for Girls pictured on page 164 of the 1909 Syllabus, saying that although the dress was optional it could be made in needlework classes from patterns which rarely exceeded 4/- in cost. The girls could wear the dress to school, changing their shoes or boots for plimsoles, which could also be bought.[2] However, the Superintendent was apparently taken to task over his support for the official version of the Girls' School Dress, when, in his next report,[3] he acknowledged that a suitable costume, and *almost* better than that previously recommended, consisted of a blue jersey and blue serge kilted skirt.[4] Boys, too, could choose to adopt the use of plimsoles on an optional basis, since many of them wore either heavy boots or were ill-shod.

In spite of the fact that the Superintendent had organised the seven teachers' classes at Kingston between 18 November 1910 and 23 June 1910, nevertheless, he organised a one-off session of instruction at Kingston on the 16 December 1910. It is not entirely clear whether or not this was a demonstration class of some kind, since several HMIs and 225 teachers were in attendance, 165 of the latter already holding the County Certificate.[5]

However, that class did not signal the end of PT classes for teachers as a further three classes were arranged by Captain Mignon to begin on 2, 6 and 7 February and terminating on 24, 25 and 27 July, respectively. The classes were held at the Central Hall, East Street School, Farnham; the Central Hall, the Council School, Roke and the Drill Hall, Dorking. Results were:-

	Attendance	Already held Certificates	Numbers who passed	Certificates	Endorsed
Farnham					
2-2-11	19 men	5	7	7	
to					
27-7-11	62 women	16	31	20	11
Roke					
6-2-11	24 men	10	17	9	8
to					
24-7-11	92 women	34	54	31	23

Dorking					
7-2-11	29 men	10	15	6	9
to					
25-7-11	67 women	23	41	21	20
Totals					
Men	72	25	39	22	17
Women	221	73	126	72	54
	293				

Some of those attending at Roke and Dorking were secondary school teachers.[6]

It is not exactly or immediately clear who or what the nature of the endorsement was since Colonel Fox had been knighted during 1910 and had been replaced by Lieutenant-Commander F H Grenfell, as HMI of PT at the Board. He had accompanied Captain Mignon on his visits to schools from the 6 July to 12 July 1911.[7]

Four more classes were organised by Captain Mignon, which he designated as six-month courses; one of them at Lingfield from 16 October 1911, another two at Wimbledon from 17 October 1911 and a further one at Richmond from the 19 October 1911. Attendances were 46, 156 and 102, respectively.

Since the beginning of his appointment three[8] years previously, twenty-two classes training 1,623 teachers had been held while in the previous three and a half years nineteen classes had been held training 1,723 teachers. The twenty refresher courses had trained 1,628 teachers.

It should be noted that the SCC issued a handbook in 1912 that designated aspects of the curriculum to be followed in elementary schools. The PT curriculum may be read at Appendix XVIII.

Sergeant Mills was appointed to Cheshire Lea on the 24 July 1912 and assumed his duties there on 1 September 1912.[9]

The replacement for Sergeant Mills was Miss Olga Haake, who had been interviewed with sixty-nine others on 25 October 1912 for the post of Assistant Instructress as from 18 November 1912. Miss Haake was trained at the Anstey PT College and had spent one year as Organizing Mistress of the West Riding County Council. Her salary on appointment was £120 rising by £10 a year to £150 p.a. However, Miss Haake resigned on 31 March 1913 and the salary advertised for her successor was £150.[10]

Sixty-five applications were received in response to Miss Haake's resignation. Eight candidates were interviewed on 19 March 1913.

Miss Dorothy Le Couteur was selected as the Assistant Instructress of PT and confirmed in the post on a salary of £150 p.a.[11]

Notes

1. SHC, Appendix H.7, Report of the Superintendent of PT, dd. 15 November 1910, pp. 733-5 in *36th Report of the SEC*, dd. 10 January 1911, pp.665-794.
2. SHC, Appendix E.3, Schedule B, Report of the Superintendent of PT, dd. 23 November 1910, pp. 773-85, in ibid., *36th Report*.
3. SHC, Appendix E.3, Schedule C, Report of the Superintendent of PT, dd. 2 November 1911, pp. 878 in *37th Report of the SEC*, dd. 14 March 1911, pp. 795-966.

4. SHC, ibid., Appendix H.2, Report of the Superintendent of PT, dd. 16 January 1911, pp. 858 in ibid., *37th Report*.
5. Ibid.
6. SHC, Appendix H.10, Report of the Superintendent of PT, 6 October 1911, pp. 465-7 in *40th Report of the SEC*, dd. 14 November 1911, pp. 363-604.
7. SHC, Schedule C, Appendix E.2, Report of the School Management Sub-Committee, pp. 495-509 in ibid., *40th Report*.
8. SHC, Appendix H.3, Report of the Superintendent of PT, dd. 23 November 1911, pp. 661-3 in *41st Report of the SEC*, 9 January 1912, pp. 605-95.
9. SHC, Appendix H. 11, Report of the Superintendent of PT, dd. 7 October 1912, pp.509 in *45th Report of the SEC*, dd. 12 November 1912.
10. SHC, Report of the Finance and General Purposes Committee, pp. 765-72 in *47th Report of the SEC*, dd. 11 March 1913.
11. SHC, Report of the Finance and General Purposes Committee, p. 99 in *48th Report of the SEC*, 22 May 1913.

CHAPTER 18
THE DEATH OF LIEUTENANT-COLONEL MIGNON

Jep(h)son George Mignon was born in Hyderabad, India in 1871. He died in action at Bezentin, France on the 14 July 1916. (The date is quoted as 14, 15 or 16 July 1916 by various sources. Some sources also include the letter "h" in his name). He was buried at Thiepval Memorial, Department de la Somme, Picardie, France. (Plot: pier and face 2C and 3A)

He was the eldest son of Colonel May Jephson George Mignon and his mother Isabella M L Mignon. He married Florence Emily Hill in 1893.

On the 22 May 1891, Gentleman cadet Jephson George Mignon from the Military College was promoted to 2nd Lieutenant/Ensign, upgraded to lieutenant on 1 December 1893 and was appointed captain on 21 March 1900.

He had fought in the Boer War when he was Staff Captain in the Imperial Yeomanry. He was awarded the Campaign Medal and the Queen's South Africa Medal with four clasps; Cape Colony, Orange Free State, Transvaal and South Africa 1901. From 10 May1902 he was placed on the Reserve of Officers as a captain in the Leicestershire Regiment.

In September 1914 he was appointed as a Major and second in command of a Service Battalion. In July 1915 he became Lieutenant-Colonel of another battalion in the Leicestershire Regiment.

All the newly created divisions recruited by Kitchener's call to arms on 5 August 1914 moved to France from August 1915. The 6th, 7th, 8th and 9th (Service) Battalions of the Leicester's formed part of Kitchener's new volunteer army and formed the 110th Brigade initially part of the 37th Division and transferred to the 21st Division on 7 July 1916.

On the first day of the Somme offensive, 1 July 1916, the 110th Brigade were still in the trenches to the north at Gommecourt and were used to provide diversions to distract German attention away from the main assault. However, the 63rd Brigade of the 21st Division was so badly decimated in the offensive, it had to be withdrawn to rebuild. As a consequence, the 110th Brigade was transferred to the 21st Division and marched south into the vicinity of Bottom Wood (Copse).

On the night of 13/14 July, the four Leicestershire Battalions moved into position through Mametz Wood onto the eastern edge, which was to be the start line. At 3:25am the British artillery barrage opened up on German positions in Villa Trench. At the same time the Leicesters headed over the top. They were met by machine gun fire. Nevertheless, by late afternoon, the Brigade were in control of Forest Trench, which was the second objective of the attack. By 7pm the last Germans had been driven out of Bazentin-le-petit-Wood.

So, although the Leicesters were successful in all four of their objectives, the Battle of Bazentin Ridge was disastrous for the battalion. About 2,000 casualties were suffered in the Brigade of about 3,300 effectives. However, a very large proportion of the casualties were fatal, particularly among the officers. Of the writer's (Kelly's) own old battalion, those officers he had known best had been killed or badly wounded.[1]

'Of the others, I grieved particularly over Colonel Mignon of the 8th battalion, one of the most charming of the many fine men I knew through the war, who was killed while leading a bombing party like a subaltern, and I remember vividly seeing him lying on his back still clutching a rifle.'[2]

The Battle of Bazentin Ridge demonstrated the problematic of the Pals' Battalions in Kitchener's New Army, the consequence of which was the incredible number of casualties suffered by so many local communities in the War's aftermath.

Newspaper reports noted he was killed on 16 July 1916 at the age of forty-five. He met his death gallantly by leading his regiment. His general wrote:

'We have lost a comrade, a brave officer and a very gallant gentleman'[3]

His chaplain was equally gracious:

'He was so loved by his men that they would have followed him anywhere and done anything for him'[4]

At a meeting of the SCC on Tuesday 25 July 1916, H.A. Powell, Chairman of the Education Committee noted that Captain Mignon had re-entered the Army as a Captain and was raised to the command of a battalion. He met his death in the same glorious way that many other officers and men had done. His death was a great blow to the Committee and would also be deeply regretted by teachers throughout the County.

Lieutenant-Colonel Mignon was awarded the Star medal and Allied Victory Medal in 1915. They were posthumously awarded to Florence Emily Mignon on 25 May 1922.

Lieutenant Colonel J G Mignon

OFFICERS 9th (SERVICE) BATTALION, THE LEICESTERS.—Back row (from left to right): Lieut. A. C. N. M. Phillips de Lisle, Sec.-Lieut. S. T. Hartshorne, Sec.-Lieut. P. E. Bent, Sec.-Lieut. W. A. Barrand, Sec.-Lieut. W. J. Wright, Sec.-Lieut. H. J. Barrand, Sec.-Lieut. C. E. N. Logan, Sec.-Lieut. O. J. Hargraves, Sec.-Lieut. G. G. Hargraves, Lieut. A. V. Poyser (R.A.M.C.). Third row: Lieut. H. F. C. Anderson, Lieut. A. S. Bennett, Sec.-Lieut. F. A. Barrett, Sec.-Lieut. S. W. Sheldon, Sec.-Lieut. B. de H. Pickard, Sec.-Lieut. H. S. Rosen, Sec.-Lieut. F. E. Papprill, Sec.-Lieut. F. C. Warner, Sec.-Lieut. M. L. Hardyman, Sec.-Lieut. F. Cresswell, Sec.-Lieut. H. Y. Martin, Lieut. H. E. Milburn, Sec.-Lieut. A. G. E. Bowell. Second row: Capt. J. B. Baxter, Capt. A. W. L. Trotter, Capt. C. R. Dibben, Capt. G. C. I. Hervey, Major J. G. Mignon (2nd in command), Col. H. R. Mead, Major R. B. Unwin, Capt. and Adjt. F. N. Harston, Capt. A. E. Boucher, Capt. F. H. Emmet, Lieut. and Qr. Mr. W. Hunt. Front row: Lieut. G. E. G. Tooth, Sec.-Lieut. A. A. D. Lee, Sec.-Lieut. F. Scott, Lieut. H. M. Henwood.

Leicestershire Regiment Officers 9th Btn The War Illustrated Vol 8 Page 2855

Gethsemane 1914-1918

The Garden called Gethsemane
In Picardy it was,
And there the people came to see
The English soldiers pass.
We used to pass
Or halt, as it might be,
And ship our masks in case of gas
Beyond Gethsemane.

The Garden called Gethsemane
It held a pretty lass,
But all the time she talked to me
I prayed my cup might pass.
The Officer sat on the chair,
The men lay on the grass,
And all the time we halted there
I prayed my cup might pass.

It didn't pass-It didn't pass-
It didn't pass from me.
I drank it when we met the gas
Beyond Gethsemane!

Kipling, Rudyard. *Rudyard Kipling. The Complete Verse*, 80-81, Kyle Cathie Limited, 2006, London.

Notes

1. Kelly, D V, (Captain Leicestershire Regiment). *39 Months with the "Tigers" 1915-1918*, 1930, 25-33, Ernest Benn Limited, London, p.32. (This publication was printed by The Naval and Military Press Ltd. No date for the reprint is quoted.); a map of the location of the battle may be found on page 26.
2. Ibid.
3. *The Times*, 7 August 1916, 14.
4. Ibid.

Other References:
The Surrey Times, 28 July 1916, 4.
Army and Navy Gazette 29 July 1916, 488.
Census for England and Wales:1881;1891;1911
Registry of Births, Marriages and Deaths
UK Commonwealth War Graves 1914-1921
England and Wales National Probate Calendar (Index of Wills and Administrations) 1858-1966
International Wargraves..Record Added 23 November 2005
Medal Roll (National Archives WO 100 Series)
British Army WW1 Medal Roll Index Cards 1914-1920
Great Western Railway Shareholders 1835-1932

CHAPTER 19
1916 AND AFTER

As a result of Colonel Mignon's death, Miss Dorothy Le Couteur, the Assistant Superintendent, was appointed as Organiser of PT on the County Inspection Staff as from 1 January 1917. Her salary was increased to £200. Miss Le Couteur was under the general supervision of the County Inspector.[1] (*see* Appendix XVII)

A consequence of Miss Le Couteur's appointment as an Organiser of PT was that the SEC received a grant of not more than half of her salary and her travelling expenses from the Board of Education, who recognised her as an Organiser. The regulations of the Board were, however, such that consultations had to take place between the SMO and the Elementary Committee.[2]

This incentive was based in accordance with *Circular 976*[3] entitled, *Grants in Aid of the Organisation and Supervision of the Teaching of PT in PES*. The essence of *Circular 976* was that PT was best done by teachers in the schools and although there had been substantial progress since the advent of the 1909 Syllabus, standards varied considerably throughout the country.

The physique of children was often unsatisfactory, malnutrition was common and the children were taught in large classes. Apparatus was not required although games, singing games, skipping, dancing, *et al.*, should be considered in addition to the free-standing movements of Swedish drill.

In 1909 PT in Training Colleges was voluntary and formed no part of the Board's Final examination for students in Training Colleges.

Leas had done much to provide classes in PT. As well as teacher classes for the general exercises, classes were also held in Folk and National Dancing and in Playground and Indoor Games. Additionally, vacation courses in PT had been conducted for several years during August, which had been supported by Maintenance Allowances for the last two years.

Nevertheless, in spite of these factors and the advances made in PT, standards still required to be raised. To meet the difficulties involved, some Leas had appointed Organisers and Supervisors of PT that enabled teachers to receive special assistance where required.

The Board were favourably impressed with the work done by these Organisers and were, therefore, prepared to encourage their extension through grants in aid of the expenditure.[4]

The duties of the Organiser of PT in PES included formal physical exercises, dancing, organised games and play and swimming. The Organiser would not be responsible for any regular teaching. Their duties were basically formulated as inspectors of teachers conducting lessons to give advice and make suggestions on completion of the lesson observation. Nevertheless, demonstration lessons might be given but any demonstration or supervision of such classes would not qualify for grant.

Moreover the Organiser would not conduct her duties autonomously. He/she had to cooperate with the SMO and the SMS relative to the training of children suffering from definite physical defects but also to the prevention of avoidable defects by means of exercises correctly taught or applied.

As a consequence the employment of an Organiser had to be approved by the Board, previous experience of PES conditions being an essential qualification. Knowledge of the Swedish system of exercises was also a necessary condition of employment as an Organiser with the desirable qualities of personal experience in the teaching of children of all ages.

Subsequently, Sir George Newman issued a circular[5] to Leas, employing Women Organisers of PT, to inform them of a course, which appeared to be managerial in content, to conduct their work more effectively. The course included lectures, demonstrations and practical instruction on PT. The course was dedicated to the instruction of teachers in PES, which included physical exercises for younger children, country and folk dances, indoor and playground games, play centres and remedial treatment. The course was scheduled for Wednesday 17 July 1918.

In 1919, the Board issued a *Revised Syllabus of Physical Exercises*[6] along with two supplementary pamphlets. This 1919 Syllabus entitled *Syllabus of Physical Training for Schools, 1919*, although previously for use in PES, could also be used in Secondary and Continuation Schools.

The circular emphasised the importance of a daily period of PT. That daily period could be used as an exercise lesson, for organised games and play (preferably on a playing field) or for swimming. There should not be less than three school lessons each week in addition to games and swimming.

An equipped gymnasium was unnecessary for PES. There ought to be enough available space for exercises and games. However, a supply of small apparatus, such as balls or bean bags was a suitable addition to the educational work of PT. Suitable clothing and footwear was a necessary condition of PT lessons, where it was possible.

The contents of the new 1919 Syllabus were:-

			Page
Prefatory Memorandum			3
Chapter			
	I	Introduction	6
	II	General Directions to Teachers	25
	III	Description of Simple Exercises And Positions	34
	IV	General Activity Exercises	
		Part I Marching, Running, Jumping etc.	65
		Part II Games(organisation)	84
	V	The Arrangements of the Class	99
	VI	Adaptations of Physical Exercises To Special Conditions	106
	VII	Physical Exercises For Children Under Seven Years Of Age	110
	VIII	Tables Of Exercises with Introduction	125
Appendices			
	A.	Suitable Clothing For Lessons In Physical Exercises	213
	B.	The Arrangement Of The General Activity Exercises In The Lesson	215
	C.	School Dancing	220
	D.	Swimming	225
Index of Contents			227

Notes

1. SHC, *66th Report of the SEC*, dd 9 January 1917, 20.
2. SHC, *68th Report of the SEC*, dd 31 July 1917, pp. 469-528, 495.
3. Board of Education, *Circular 976, Grants in Aid of the Organization and Supervision of the Teaching of Physical Training in Public Elementary Schools*, dd. 10 February 1917, pp. 1-3.
4. Ibid., para 8.
5. Board of Education, Medical Department, *Circular 1029, Circular to Local Education Authorities employing Women Organisers of Physical Training*, dd 16 February 1918, 1 of 1.
6. Board of Education, *Circular 1138, Revised Syllabus of Physical Exercises*, Circular to Local Education Authorities, dd 12 December 1919, 1 of 2.

CHAPTER 20
CONCLUSION

This essay has two distinct but inter-related themes. The first might suggest that certain personalities involved with the development of PT in Surrey's Public Elementary Schools were possibly pre-eminent, and, perhaps, even harbingers of the development of the Model Course in PT in 1902. The evidence is, perhaps, slight, but plausible, considering the available evidence.

Surrey schools were certainly a favourite inspection place for Colonel Fox's visits. On 8 May 1903, for instance, Colonel Fox, who was then ensconced as "Inspector of Physical Training to the Education Department"[1] visited Goldsworth Council School along with J C Colvill and the "Inspector of Physical Training for Scotland".* They saw classes I and II go through some of their exercises. All expressed their pleasure at the drill they saw.

On 10 July 1903[2] it was recorded that on the previous day (Thursday) the "Most Honourable, The Marquis of Londonderry KG, President of the Board of Education visited the school along with Colonel Fox, J C Colvill and a number of Ladies and Gentlemen". The object of the visit was to see the children go through their physical exercises, but, owing to lack of time, only two sections of the infants were able to drill before his Lordship. Nevertheless, he expressed pleasure at what he saw and regretted he was unable to see the whole. Here the narrative ends but it seems reasonably clear that what they witnessed was drill according to the Model Course, and, speculation might suggest that some of the teachers at the school had attended the courses at which 677 teachers had attended (see Chapter 2).

The second theme is that of the practical steps taken by Major Norman and Captain Mignon to implement the 1904 Syllabus in terms of a large rural county, Surrey.

Physical Training was carried out in all sorts of places varying from the central hall to the small and over-crowded classroom. In most schools facilities were adequate. A few, however, were unable to provide adequate facilities during wet weather. Playgrounds were generally suitable for PT though most needed remetalling, a day's rain making them unfit for use.[3]

The best guide was the *Departmental Committee on Playgrounds*, 1912. Mr. P F Story, Surveyor to the SEC, considered tar-paving as a preferable surface to gravel and ash and clinker in playgrounds, since it was usable after rain, was less injurious to children when they fell and was not prone to cause throat infections during hot weather in the summer. He also reported the Superintendent as considering that, for the Board of Education's 1909 Syllabus to be properly effected, a space of fifty feet with a minimum of twenty feet was the least that would

---

* An Inspector of Physical Training for Scotland did not exist until 1905 when Captain Parker, was appointed as Inspector of Physical Instruction. This reference may have referred to Sir Henry Craik, Secretary of the Scottish Education Department, who seems to have accompanied Colonel Fox and J C Colvill on some of these visits.

suffice for a class of fifty children. Mr. Story also submitted a table showing those schools, excluding passages and narrow spaces in the playground, which had a nett allowance of less than thirty square feet per head in the playground:[4]

Departments of	Under 5 sq. ft.	5-10 sq. ft	10-15 sq.ft	15-20 sq. ft	20-25 sq.ft	25-30 sq.ft
Council Schools	-	4	-	4	3	4
Voluntary Schools	8 (7 of which were nil)	9	8	19	11	3

It seems clear that the improvement in surfacing by tar-paving, which in Surrey cost 3/2d per square yard, accounts to some extent for the rise in activity not only for physical exercises as prescribed by the 1909 Syllabus but also in games like netball, which needed reasonable surfacing to develop the game.

As a result of his visits, Major Norman made various recommendations. All but one were recommended for adoption by the Special Committeee.[5] All teachers had to pass through a class of instruction and even physically unfit teachers had to be acquainted with the theoretical aspects of the exercises. A uniform system of training based on the 1904 Syllabus was gradually adopted so that the instruction of teachers could work its way through. Swimming** was also encouraged as a curriculum subject taking up part of the time given to PT. Classes in physical exercises were arranged for the evening schools.

Of all the recommendations in *circular 515*, the training of teachers was most important. A uniform system of training was established in the pupil teacher centres, the secondary schools and the elementary schools.[6]

The most immediate training requirement was for those in post, which, first established by Major Norman, was subsequently developed by Captain Mignon, who, was also responsible for the development in Surrey schools of the 1909 Syllabus issued by the Board of Education. The incentive of certification offered to teachers was a springboard to increased proficiency and efficiency, although the Board of Education refused to become involved. Moreover, they raised the status of physical education as a practical subject because it had become more than a means of enforcing discipline and organisation. Teachers who became "qualified" were actively engaged in the teaching of a scientific technique of instruction for the improvement in the health and welfare of the elementary school child.

Nevertheless, it is difficult to escape the conclusion that these aims were possibly undermined by several factors, one of which, is to assess, for instance, whether or not the concept of all teachers attending the classes was realised bearing in mind the objections, vociferously voiced, by some members of the profession to the initial appointment of Major Norman (*see* Appendix XII). However, this factor may be said to have been mitigated by the system of inspection, which meant that schools had to maintain a reasonable standard of efficiency in drill. Colonel Fox's participation in this process enhanced the perception of its importance as a curriculum subject.

** *In the Swim. The Origins and Systematic Development of Children's Swimming in the County of Surrey's Public Elementary Schools 1905-1921 Pioneered by Major Arthur Ormand Norman: A Documentary History with Various Appendices Including Swimming and Washing Verminous Children in the London School Board.* Vol. 3. by J Robert Pegg, Angela Blaydon Publishing Ltd, 2017.

One of the most difficult aspects to implement was the amount of curriculum time spent on PT, which, in 1905 varied considerably from school to school.[7] This situation was resolved in 1908 by the Special Committee of the Consultative Board.[8]

Solve one problem, however, and another appears. By September 1907 Major Norman complained that many exercises were too instructional. More schools should attempt more advanced work.[9] It was in this context that Captain Mignon introduced the notion of emulation. Those of low ability should emulate those of higher ability through the introduction of "sections".

In one sense, therefore, the presentation of Swedish drill as a scientific process designed to increase the health and welfare of the elementary school child illustrated the tensions exhibited in the discipline and organisation factors that were more fundamentally intrinsic to military drill. Nevertheless, one cannot ignore George Newman's support, as CMO of the SMS, for the former idea of Swedish drill as a scientific, health and welfare project.[10]

On a general level of interest it has been suggested[11] that body management, of which one supposes that Swedish Drill formed a part, draws on Foucault's[12] arguments that promoted disciplinary techniques played out in the specific context of British history from the late Victorian period to the end of the 1930s and why this mattered politically. Body management in that sense relates to expanding Government practice and popular self-help schemes, such as those promoted by *Sandow, et al.* A well-managed body was not only the goal of social policy but also an integral aspect of fashioning the self. In these senses, a healthy and fit body was seen as a sign of responsible citizenship.[13] In some ways, therefore, the belief in an elitist, technocratic, top-down structure, such as that of Swedish Drill as a mediating factor in the fitness of the nation by the likes of Sir George Newman may have had wider repercussions, insofar as it had the "empowering potential of creating new possibilities".[14] In that sense, it was an enabling power insofar as it expanded the range of people's choices and, as a result, shaped patterns of social behavior more broadly in the context of the beneficial attributes of Public Health.

It should always be borne in mind that the 1903, 1904 and 1905 Reports and the establishment of the SMS were crucially influential in the establishment of Swedish drill as the perceived exemplar of physical exercise in the health improvement of the elementary school child above that of the games ethic. The fact that in Surrey's PES the impetus was undertaken by former Army officers is, in a sense, beside the point. There can be no question of their dedication, interest and enthusiasm for the introduction and implementation of Swedish drill as a scientific, curriculum subject that displayed all the outward appearances of a militaristic framework.

The fact was that, in essence, with large classes, variable playground and indoor facilities, and, only a slowly developing notion of a separate dress for physical training, there was great enthusiasm among teachers, particularly women, who outnumbered men in all the courses undertaken by Major Norman and Captain Mignon, in a participatory process of perceived health improvement in their pupils.

Notes

1. The Log Book of Goldsworth School, Woking, 8 May 1903, pp. 76.
2. Ibid., 10 July 1903, pp. 78.
3. SHC, Appendix E.3, Report of the Superintendent of PT, dd 21 December 1905, pp. 333-43 in, *13th Report of the SEC*, pp. 169-449.

4. Board of Education, *Report of the Departmental Committee on Playgrounds*, 1912, 96.
5. SHC, Appendix E.1, Report of the Special Committee on Physical Training and Medical Inspection, dd 21 December 1905, pp. 319-20 in op. cit., *13th Report*.
6. SHC, Appendix E.3, op. cit., 333-343 in ibid., *13th Report.*
7. Ibid.
8. SHC, Appendix E. 1, Report of the Special Sub-Committee appointed to consider the Curriculum of Elementary Schools, dd 26 February 1908, pp.326-34 in *24th Report of the SEC*, dd 28 July 1908, 332.
9. SHC, Appendix E.2, Report of the Superintendent of PT, dd 7 September 1907, pp. 1972-4 in *21st Report of the SEC*, dd 12 November 1907, pp.1839-2080.
10. McIntosh, Peter C. *Physical Education in England since 1800*, 158, Bell & Hyman Ltd., Revised Edition 1968.
11. Zweiniger-Bargielowska, Ina. *Managing the Body, Beauty, Health and Fitness in Britain 1880-1939*, 7, OUP, 2010.
12. Foucault, Michel. *Discipline and Punish, The Birth of the Prison*, 149-50, Peregrine Books, 1977.
13. Pegg, J Robert. *Quick March! To Athletic Sports: The Origins and Development of Drill, Athletics, Cricket, Football and Swimming in Croydon's Elementary Schools 1893-1910: A Newspaper Documentary History*, 90-92, abpublishing, Revised edition 2016.
14. Zweiniger-Bargielowska, Ina, op.cit., 7-8.

Plate I. The Grave of Major Norman in Haslemere Cemetery
Photo © the author

Plate II. Lieutenant Colonel Mignon
Reproduced by kind permission of Digital Preservation Leicestershire,
Leicester and Rutland Record Office

Plate III. Lieutenant Colonel Mignon
Reproduced by kind permission of Digital Preservation Leicestershire,
Leicester and Rutland Record Office

Plate IV. Lieutenant Colonel Mignon
Reproduced by kind permission of Digital Preservation Leicestershire,
Leicester and Rutland Record Office

*Plate V. Officers of the 8th Battalion, The Leicestershire Regisment
Reproduced by kind permission of Digital Preservation Leicestershire,
Leicester and Rutland Record Office*

Plate VI. The 8th Leicestershire Regisment
By kind permission of Digital Preservation Leicestershire, Leicester and Rutland Record Office

Plate VII. The 8th Leicestershire Regiment
By kind permission of Digital Preservation Leicestershire, Leicester and Rutland Record Office

Plate VIII. Thiepval Memorial, Thiepval
Departement de la Somme
Picardie, France
Plot: Pier and Face 2 C and 3 A

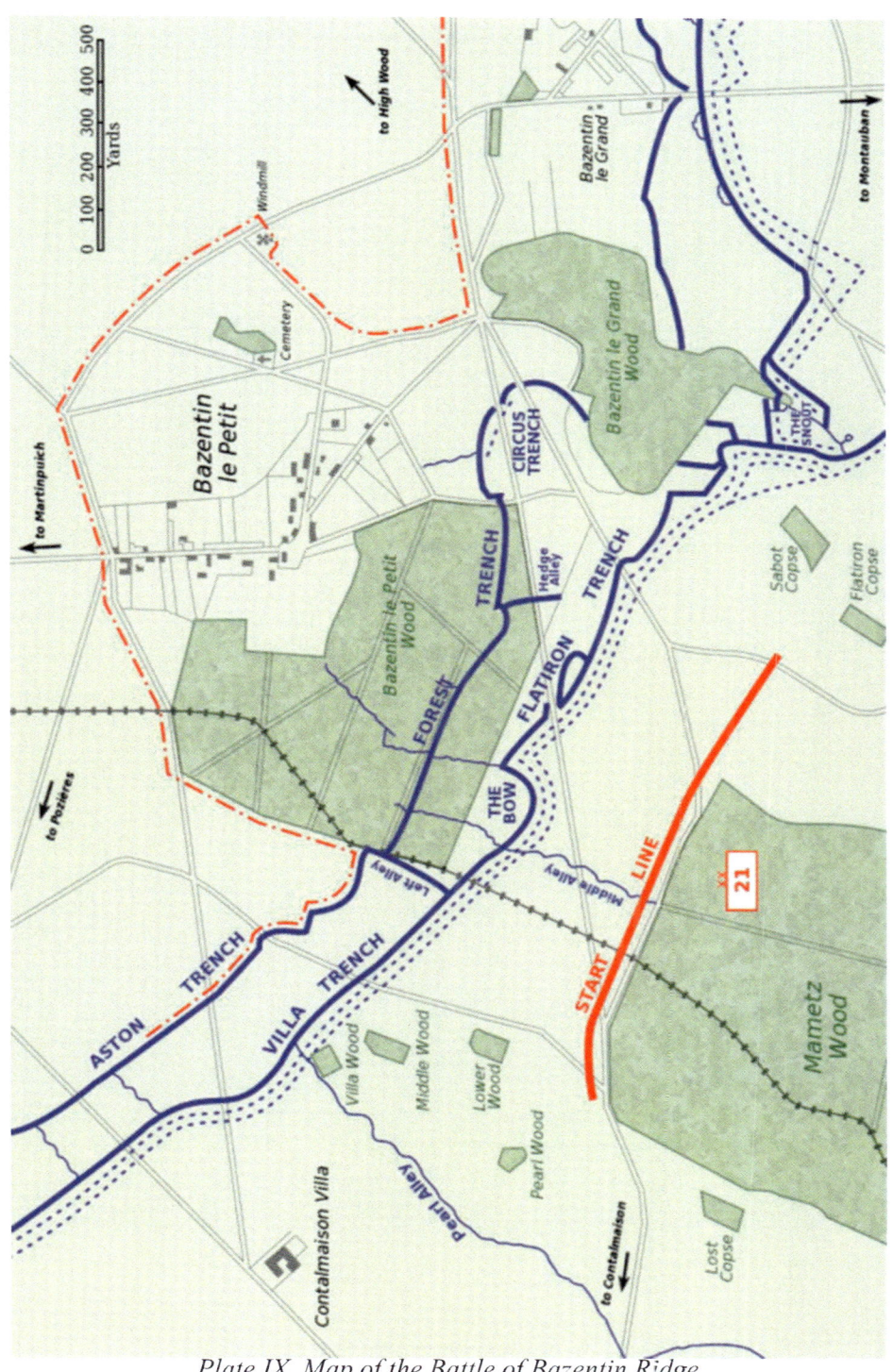

Plate IX. Map of the Battle of Bazentin Ridge
From Call to Arms : Leicesters and The Battle of Bazentin Ridge
German trenches = solid blue line
Barbed wire defences = broken blue line

Plate X. Colonel Fox
Colonel Sir George Malcolm Fox (1843–1918)
by unknown artist
Oil on canvas, 101.6 x 81.3 cm

Reproduced courtesy of The Royal Army Physical Training Corps Museum, Aldershot

Plate XI. Colonel Fox
From Bailey's Magazine of Sports and Pastimes
No. 670 December 1915 Vol. CIV

Plate XII. Colonel Fox in Vanity Fair
A Vanity Fair Print of Col George Malcolm Fox Dated Sept 3rd 1896 The Caption Reads " Swordsmanship "
This is a faithful photographic reproduction of a two-dimensional, public domain work of art. The work of art itself is in the public domain for the following reason:
This work is in the public domain in those countries with a copyright term of life of the author plus 90 years or less.
This reproduction has been identified as being free of known restrictions under copyright law, including all related and neighbouring rights

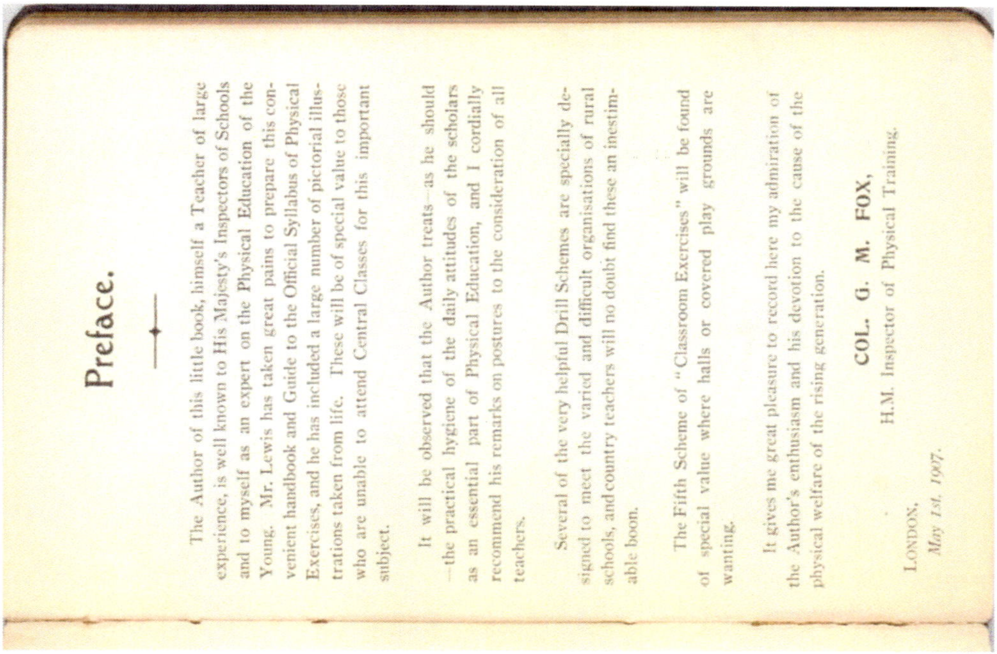

Preface.

The Author of this little book, himself a Teacher of large experience, is well known to His Majesty's Inspectors of Schools and to myself as an expert on the Physical Education of the Young. Mr. Lewis has taken great pains to prepare this convenient handbook and Guide to the Official Syllabus of Physical Exercises, and he has included a large number of pictorial illustrations taken from life. These will be of special value to those who are unable to attend Central Classes for this important subject.

It will be observed that the Author treats – as he should – the practical hygiene of the daily attitudes of the scholars as an essential part of Physical Education, and I cordially recommend his remarks on postures to the consideration of all teachers.

Several of the very helpful Drill Schemes are specially designed to meet the varied and difficult organisations of rural schools, and country teachers will no doubt find these an inestimable boon.

The Fifth Scheme of "Classroom Exercises" will be found of special value where halls or covered play grounds are wanting.

It gives me great pleasure to record here my admiration of the Author's enthusiasm and his devotion to the cause of the physical welfare of the rising generation.

COL. G. M. FOX,
H.M. Inspector of Physical Training.

LONDON,
May 1st, 1907.

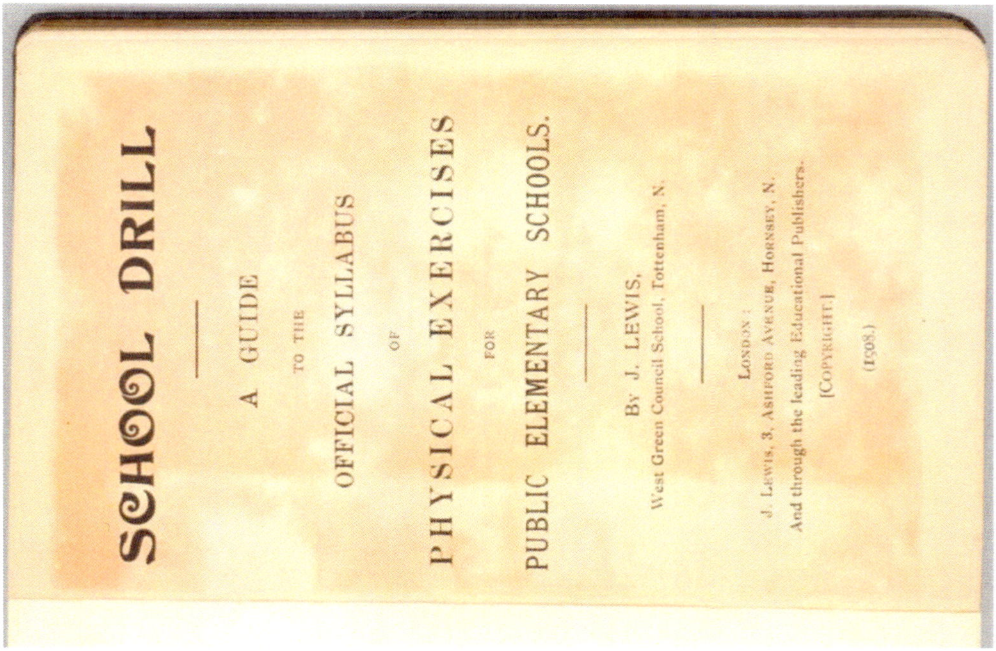

SCHOOL DRILL

A GUIDE
TO THE
OFFICIAL SYLLABUS
OF
PHYSICAL EXERCISES
FOR
PUBLIC ELEMENTARY SCHOOLS.

By J. LEWIS,
West Green Council School, Tottenham, N.

LONDON:
J. LEWIS, 3, ASHFORD AVENUE, HORNSEY, N.
And through the leading Educational Publishers.
[COPYRIGHT.]

(1908.)

Plate XIII. Fox`s endorsement of this "little book" as a guide to the 1904 syllabus is an interesting comment in so far as the book`s author credits HMI`s E. H. Carter and J. H. Cooke for their assistance in its subject matter and compilation

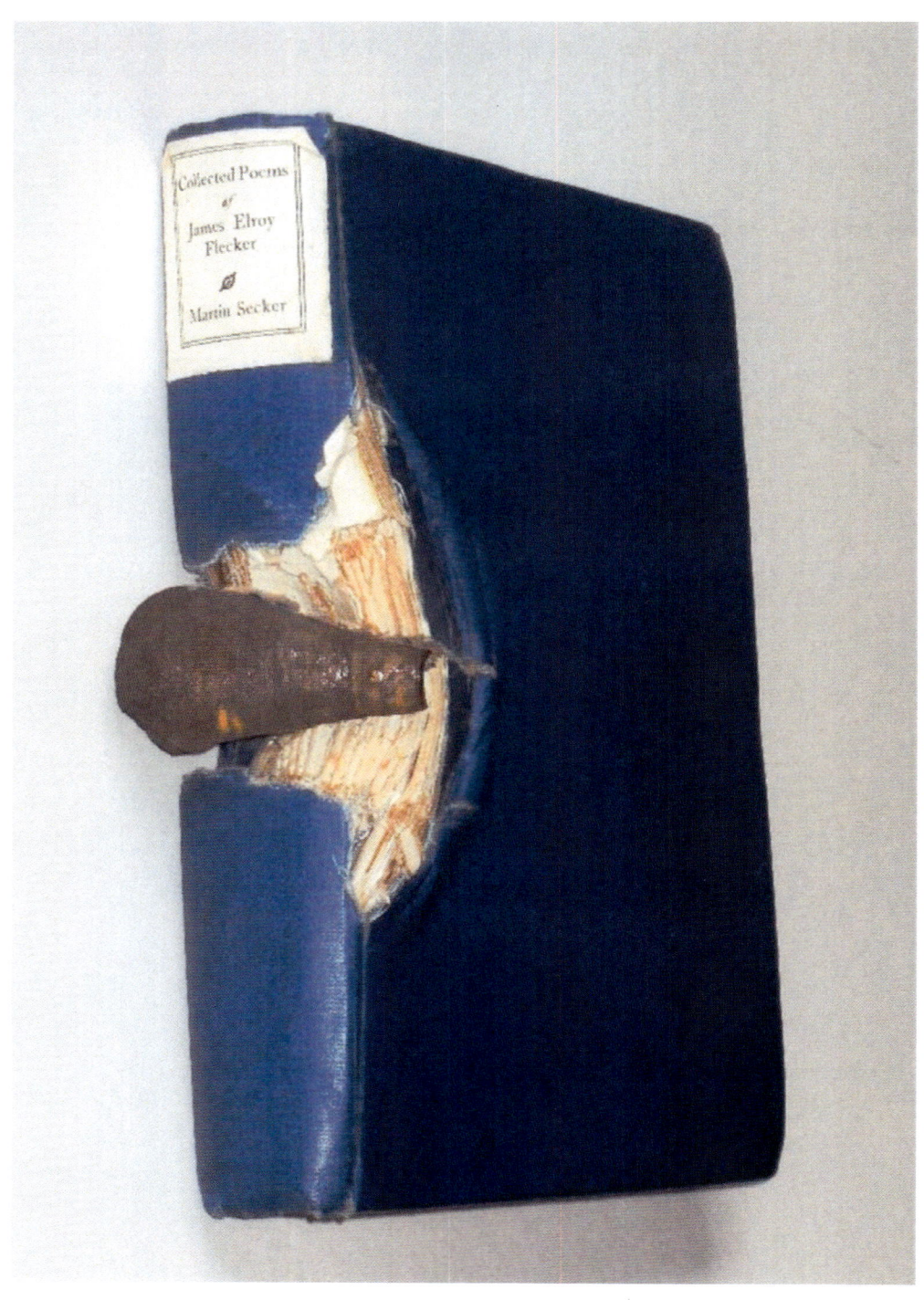

Plate XIV. German shrapnel from UB-37. In the possession of Frank Grenfell, nephew of Captain Grenfell, to whom grateful thanks are acknowledged for supplying and allowing this picture to be published

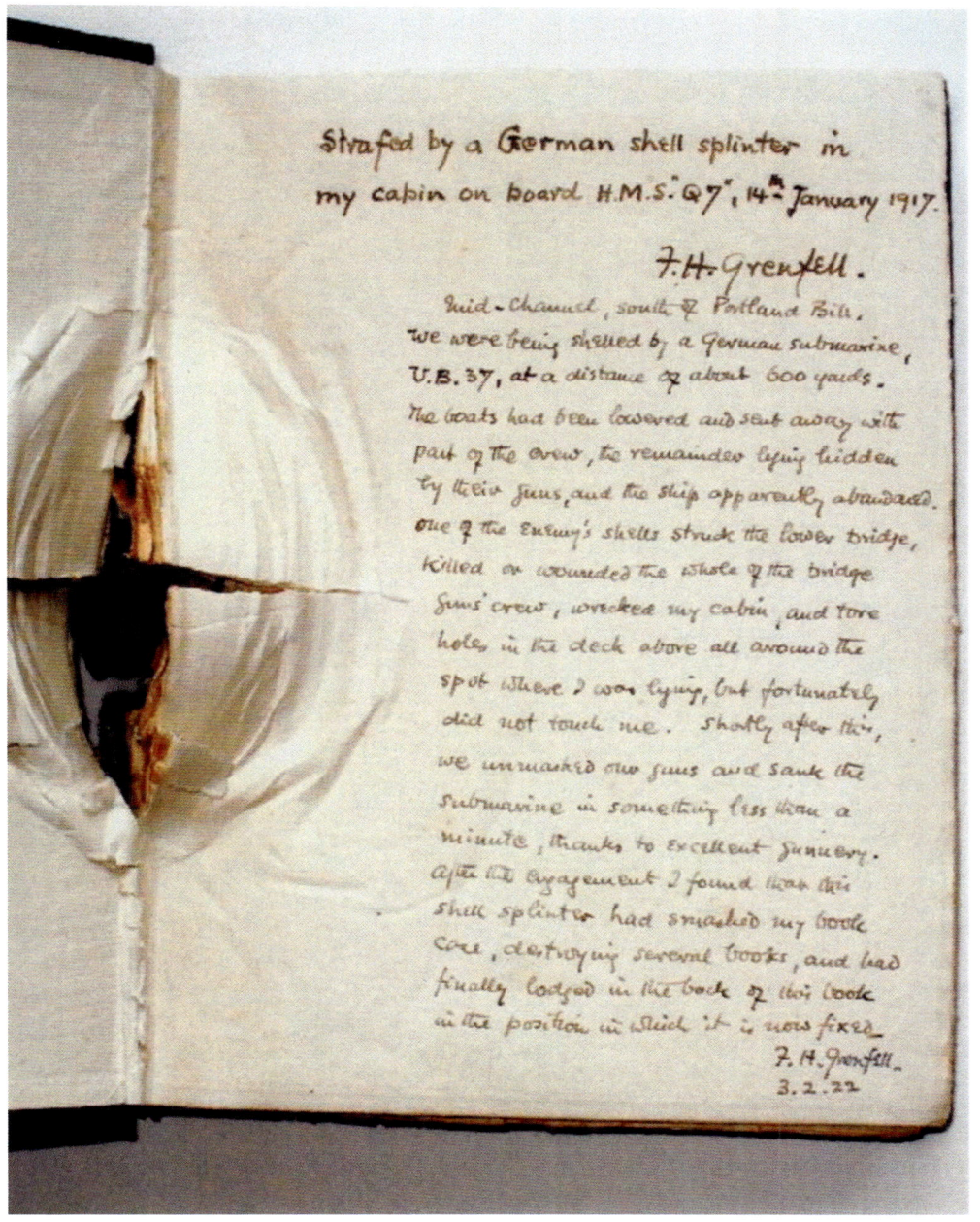

Plate XV. Written account of shrapnel incident on 14 January 1917 by Captain Grenfell.
Grateful thanks to Frank Grenfell, nephew of Captain Grenfell, for supplying and allowing use of this document for publication

Plate XVI. Tolkien's 1911 Journey
The journey points are consistent with the journey outlined in "Tolkien's Gedling" but that the route outlined may have some points of departure but is as nearly accurate as can be corroborated in view of the fact that the journey was over 100 years ago. Thanks to Greg Witt for compiling this map

APPENDIX I
LORD MEATH

"Two things are necessary for the successful inculcation of patriotism. The first is social reform, so that everyone may possess something worth fighting for; the second is the teaching in the schools of a moral and sane patriotism, which must include love of God, love of duty and love of all that is noble and which tends to raise and inspire the human heart."[1]

Reginald Brabazon, 12th Earl of Meath, was born on 31 July 1841and died on 11 October 1929 aged 88. He succeeded his father as 12th Earl on 26 May 1887.

He was educated at Eton and in Germany gaining entry by competitive examination to the Foreign Office as a clerk in 1863. He entered the Diplomatic Service in 1868, was assigned to Berlin and left for The Hague in 1870. In 1871 he passed on to Paris but retired from diplomacy in 1873, when he returned to England.

From then on he held significant administrative posts in a range of organisations. In 1874 he became Honorary Secretary of the first Hospital Saturday Council while in 1879 he was elected Chairman of the Young Men's Friendly Society. He founded the Metropolitan Public Garden Association in 1882. He was first Chairman of the British College of Physical Education. He was also first Chairman of the Parks Committee of the LCC as well as the first President of the Church Reform Association as well as the the Lads' Drill Association. President of the Church Army, the Earl of Meath held the same position with regard to the Christian Union of Social Service.

In Ireland he became first President of the Dublin Philanthropic Reform Association and, did for many years actively engage in social and philanthropic work and took an active part in the promotion of the Empire Movement.

Created a Knight of St Patrick in 1902, the Earl was Her Majesty's Lieutenant for the City of Dublin from 1898.

He was elected as an alderman of the LCC in 1887; Honorary Colonel of the 5th Militia Battalion of the Royal Dublin Fusiliers; was a knight of Justice of the Order of St John of Jerusalem in England and ex-Chancellor of the Royal University of Ireland.

He had seats at Killruddery, Bray, Ireland; The Coppice, Rothdrum, Ireland and Ottermead, Ottershaw, Chertsey, Surrey. His town house was at 83 Lancaster Gate.

He was a member of the Travellers' and Batchelors' Clubs in London and of Kildare Street Club, Dublin.

He married Lady Mary Jane Maitland in 1868, who was the only surviving daughter of the 11th Earl of Lauderdale.[2]

He stood as an example of what could be achieved by a single-minded and often single-handed, private citizen who had imagination, public spirit and pertinacity. The movements that he initiated or kept alive were innumerable. Nearly all of them were of real social value. Many of them survived in the inter-war period and were accepted as a recognised part of the national life. Hospitals, parks, open-spaces, early closing in London, physical training in schools, workshops for disabled men, cheap popular drama and Boy Scouts were all, in their turn, the object of Lord Meath's indefatigable philanthropy. He was best known for the invention of Empire Day in 1896. Under the banner of "One King, One Flag, One Fleet, One Empire"[3]

Empire Day was established as the one special day of the year when the thoughts of the nation and particularly school children, whose participation was often questioned, should celebrate the heritage passed down from their forefathers. The ideals of service and citizenship engendered in the notion and practice of Empire Day were inspirational and there could be no better memorial to him than the perpetual observance of Empire Day for generations to come.[4]

Photograph reproduced by courtesy of Modern Records Centre, University Library, University of Warwick

State Library of Queensland.
Source: Item is held by John Oxley Library, State Library of Queensland.

Notes

1. Letter from Lord Meath, "The Teaching of Patriotism" in *The Times Educational Supplement*, 7 December 1915.
2. Grant, John, Edited. *Surrey – Historical, Biographical and Pictorial*, The London and Provincial Publishing Co Ltd., 84 Hatton Garden. Published only for subscriber, no page number and no date.
3. Penn, Alan, *Targeting Schools*, 4, Woburn Press, London, 1999.
4. *The Times*, 12 October 1929, 11

APPENDIX II
A SHORT HISTORY OF PHYSICAL EDUCATION FROM ROUSSEAU TO 1904

The concept of modern physical education, physical training, gymnastic and physical exercises began with the political and educational theories of Jean-Jacques Rousseau (1712-1778). He postulated the notion of the general will as an answer to the problem of evil in the world.[1] If God was the creator of good in this world, how could God also be responsible as the creator of evil?[2] Rousseau's answer was that evil was the creation of human society.[3] The general will was the concept, therefore, of the common good into which all men must enter. Within this concept lies the inherent notion of this as what would be best for themselves as individuals[4] – *the will of all* (*see also* Barth, Karl, *From Rousseau to Ritschil*, 71-74, SCM Press Ltd, English Edition, London, 1959).

Although these concepts applied to children, he rejected every thought of original sin.[5] Children were thus born free of any taint whatsoever. It was society that repressed and enchained them. In order to pass into Society, children had to pass through various stages of development.[6] Society was a social contract:

> "all can prescribe what all must do, whereas none has the right to demand that another do anything that he himself does not do".[7]

The aims of education, therefore, were, paradoxically, not to fit the child into Society but to free *him* from its shackles,[8] so that he would not need to convince himself that he was free.[9] The paradigm of Rousseau's educational theory was epitomized in *Emile* (1762), where the exercise of the body, limbs, senses and strength were far more important than that of the mind which should be delayed as long as possible.[10]

Emile was, therefore, to be taught in the context of a system of education far removed from the existing culture. Indeed, Rousseau regarded *Emile* as a book on moral philosophy rather than an educational treatise. In essence it was a treatise on the natural goodness of mankind *where man was naturally good*.[11]

Nevertheless, the concept of transferable skills from adults to children was assessed by Rousseau as a distinct form of physical action:

> "I have sometimes asked why children are not given the same games of skill as men; tennis, mall, (i.e. *the game of pall mall played with a mallet**), billiards, archery, football and musical instruments......To dash from one of the room to another, to judge the rebound of a ball before it touches the ground, to return it with strength and accuracy, such games are are not so much sports fit for a man, as sports fit to make a man of him."[12]

*author's italics

It was, in the context of improving educational methods in the State system of education in Prussia, on the basis of his interpretation of *Emile*, that Johann Bernhard Basedow (1723-1790) opened the Philanthropium school on 27 December 1774 in Dessau in the German Duchy of Anhalt.[13]

Basedow developed a curriculum based on a variety of physical exercises as well as natural sciences and geography.[14] As time passed additional subjects were added to the curriculum by the teachers such as singing and reading aloud with a range of physical activity including dancing, marching and swimming.[15] There is a distinct sense in which this curriculum was, not only, innovative, but, also, a political and social theory since *the curriculum of a school or schools* represents all those things which are present or potentially possible in the Social construct of a school. In *Emile* the key idea was:

> "the possibility of preserving the original perfect nature of the child by means of the careful control of his education and environment, based upon an analysis of the different physical and psychological stages through which he passed from birth to maturity."[16]

In the spring of 1781 until the end of February 1784 Christian Gotthilf Salzmann (1744-1811) taught at the Dessau Philanthropium, but, desiring to implement his own ideas on the basis of his time spent at Dessau, he opened his own Philanthropium at Schnepfenthal on the estate of Duke Ernst II in the farming district of Saxe-Gotha, the foundation stone of which was laid on 18 June 1784.[17]

Johann Christoph Friedrich GutsMuths (1759-1839) was the fourth teacher at the school in Dessau but his contribution lasted almost fifty years, which places him in the forefront of developments in physical education.[18] It should be noted that the English version of GutsMuths book *Gymnastics for Youth*, 1800, was originally attributed to Salzmann, but this book was but one of a number that he wrote during his fifty years at Schnepfenthal. In *Gymnastics for Youth*, GutsMuths outlines outdoor exercises such as:

- plate 1, which demonstrates ten different figures of apparatus to be used;
- plate 2, demonstrating a leap in height with or without a pole;
- plate 3, demonstrating the leap in length with or without a pole
- plate 4, running and leap frog
- plate 5, throwing and shooting at a mark
- plate 6, the different kinds of wrestling
- plate 7, climbing
- plate 8, preservation of equilibrium
- plate 9, trundling a hoop
- plate 10, bathing and swimming
- an additional plate at the beginning of the book shows an ensemble of activities including kite flying.[19]

The pages of *Gymnastics for Youth* refer occasionally to *Emile*[20] and other works notably Claudius Galen (131-201),[21] John Locke (1632-1704)[22] and Clement Joseph Tissot (Joseph-Clement) (1750-1826)[23].

Galen, for example, notes that gymnastics includes: horsemanship, hunting with hounds, digging, reaping, woodcutting, rowing, dancing, and, in fact, all those physical activities in which people engage.[24]

Tissot's *Gymnastique Medicinale et Chirurgicale* (1780)[25] (Medicinal and Surgical Gymnastics) was sub-titled *Essay On the usefulness of Movement, or different Exercises of the body, and of rest, in the treatment of Diseases*. Tissot was born on 4 June 1747. He obtained his medical diploma in 1776. He was, therefore thirty-three when his book on therapeutic exercise was published. After various perils associated with the French Revolution he participated in military campaigns in Austria, Prussia, Poland and Italy ending up in Swabia taking care of Austrian prisoners suffering from dysentery, which he controlled with hygienic measures. From there he became Surgeon-in-Chief of the Army from 25 September 1808 to 15 June 1810. Recalled, he became chief surgeon to the military hospital at Aix-la-Chapelle from November 1810 until August 1811 when he returned to private practice. He died in 1826.[26]

Tissot's book was concerned with the medical aspects of remedial action in terms of recuperation and rehabilitation. Nevertheless, it was one of a number of books that were concerned with the importance of bodily exercise in the restoration and preservation of health.[27] His book was published in five languages: French, German, Italian, Swedish and English.

In one sense, it would appear that GutsMuths and his colleagues were able to assess the notion of health as an alternative conception of nature:

> " we must not ascribe our physical degeneracy in the least to any alteration of her (Nature's) laws, and her energy, but to contingent causes, that is, to a defective development of the germe, through the fault of our parents, and of circumstances; to deteriorating education; to a debilitating way of life; and sometimes to disadvantages of climate."[28]

These ideas seem to owe more to Charles Louis de Secondat, Baron de Montesquieu (1689-1755)[29] than to Rousseau but the notion that nature's deficiencies were remediable through physical exercise, based on the works of Galen, was crucial to the improvement of the human condition.

Nevertheless, GutsMuths clearly enunciated his principles for gymnastics which as a general theory

> "should be constructed on physiological principles, and the practice of each exercise be regulated by the physical qualities of each individual: but such perfection is not to be expected in the following work, built solely on the genuine experience of eight years practice, which has convinced me, that gymnastics are necessary to education, and that, as they are here inculcated, they are not merely innocent, but extremely beneficial both to the bodies and minds of youth."[30]

Although the ideas of GutsMuths appear to have been marginal in their influence in England, two versions of gymnastic exercises developed; one in Germany. The German Turnverein System emphasised apparatus work of a formal nature, stressing muscular development.[31] The other was by Pehr Henrik Ling (1776-1839) in Sweden, a version of free standing exercises, ostensibly founded on a scientific examination of physiological and anatomical analysis[32] but who classified his work in terms of educational, aesthetic, medical and military gymnastics.[33] Nevertheless, Ling's system failed to make much of an effect on PE in England until the appointment of Miss Concordia Lofving as Lady Superintendent of PE in 1878 to teach the Swedish system to girls in the PES of the London School Board.[34]

Ideas of physical exercise reappeared in a guise expressly, but not wholly, associated with elementary education and the Newcastle Commission.[35]

Edwin Chadwick (1800-1890), had been appointed a Poor Law Commissioner in 1833 and was secretary to the Commission as a result of the Poor Law Act, 1834. Moreover, Chadwick was an apostle of the half-time system under which working class children divided their day between school and factory which had its origins in the Factory Act, 1833. The Factory Act, 1844, reinforced the half-time system as acceptable from the educational as well as the industrial point of view.[36]

Chadwick wrote two papers on the half-time system,[37] which he submitted in evidence to the Newcastle Commission.[38] He observed that systematized drill should be introduced for three specific reasons: sanitary, moral and economical. Drill was good for the correction of congenital bodily defects. Moreover, systematized drill incorporated all those ideals inherent in the notion of discipline: duty, order, obedience to command, self-restraint, punctuality and patience.[39] Furthermore, drill improved the efficiency of the pupils, and their productive capacity with the probability of a cheap, defensive force available for the nation.[40]

Another advocate of the half-time system was Charles Dickens (1812-1870).[41] In 1863, Dickens accompanied Chadwick[42] on a visit to the Limehouse School of Industry which was run by the Guardians of the Stepney Union.[43] They operated a half-time system.[44] Dickens published a glowing account of his visit in an article *The Short Timers*.[45]

He had first watched the boys at military drill.[46] He enjoyed the military and naval precision, alertness and tidiness. The boys were bright, quick, eager and steady in perfect uniformity, yet, with an individual spirit of emulation and enjoyment. The military drill was followed by broadsword exercise then naval drill on an artificial ship with masts, yards and sails. The Mainmast was seventy feet high and the boys were experts at manning the rigging. A military band appeared and entertained.

The boys subsequently gave a good account of themselves in geography and mental arithmetic. The boys, as well as the girls, could cook, mend their clothes and clean up around them. The girls had womanly household knowledge added. The school produced an above-average number of pupil teachers. It distinguished itself well in the merchant navy, army and domestic service. Corporal punishment was unknown and the school's moral health was excellent. Nevertheless, the success of the half-time system in its early years may be attributed to the fact that it was the first State system of educational enforcement.[47] It was not until the Education Act, 1918, (1918 Act) that the half-time system was finally abolished.[48]

Chadwick's interest in "drill" did not end with the half-time system, however, for it was he who activated through the Society of Arts, a drill review of London Schools, the first of which was held at the Crystal Palace on the 21 June 1870.[49] This report suggests that 3,000 boys participated mostly from Government asylum schools, industrial schools and workhouse schools. The report appears to suggest the participation of one or two *British* elementary schools.[50]

Nor was the general view of the beneficial aspects of military drill confined to the half-time system or the working classes for it was also necessary to induce a spirit of militarism among all schoolboys preventing them from becoming round-shouldered and would offer a cure for slouching.[51] The pressure for the inclusion of a military approach to educational improvement in all schools was, therefore, formidable by the time of the 1870 Act and especially as the army had a history of inadequate healthy recruitment.

A study of army recruitment, based on the height of recruits during the period prior to 1820, concluded that apparent patterns of occupational and geographic differences in height was indicative of substantial improvement in the nutritional circumstance and general welfare of the working class. After that date, however, the working class suffered a decline in their nutritional circumstances and their general welfare. This accorded with popular perceptions apparent in the middle of the 19th century.[52]

The Crimean War, in particular, had revealed very serious defects in the British Army. The problems of army recruitment at this time, was both a rural and an urban one. The towns supplied the best educated and most intelligent men but they were the most weakly. Their constitutions failed under the hardships of military life.[53]

Nevertheless, the army was aware that other factors were responsible for the general dissipation of the recruits.[54] From 1 July 1860 to 30 June 1861, out of 2,769 discharges from Fort Pitt, 445 men (16.07%) had under two years' service. Of the 445 men, heart disease constituted 13.7% of the total and lung disease (phthisis) 34.15%. In the following year, there was a total of 40.59%, 14.76% and 25.83%, respectively. The Report of the Committee appointed to report on Gymnastic Instruction for the Army set out some important principles.[55]

Every recruit was to undergo at least a three-month course of gymnastic training at the same time as ordinary drill.[56] Medical Regulations were to demand that MOs watch the gymnastic exercises.[57] A medical inspection was to be instituted on a fortnightly basis. Trained infantrymen of ten years' service had to undergo a course of gymnastic exercises for three months of every year. Measurements of each man's height, weight, chest, forearm and upper arm[58] were recorded at the beginning and end of each course of gymnastics.[59]

The connection between military recruitment and the state of the civilian labour market was established at the end of the 19th century.[60] However, there was no index of exactitude in measuring the relationship.[61] Moreover, the alleged[62] deterioration or the inexactitude of measurement in the physical qualities of army recruits at the time of the Boer War was expanded to include the whole of the British race.[63] The conclusions of Major-General Sir Frederick Maurice ultimately led to the *1904 Report*.

Notes

1. Cassirer, Ernst. *The Question of Jean-Jacques Rousseau*, 1954, 75, translated and edited by Peter Gay, Indiana University Press, Midland Book Edition, Columbia University Press, 1963.
2. Rousseau, Jean-Jacques. *Emile*, 1762, translated by Barbara Foxley, Introduction, 5, Everyman's Library, 1911, Introduction J M Dent, 1974.
3. Ibid., and Cassirer, Ernst, op. cit., 75.
4. Jones, W T, *Masters of Political Thought, Machiavelli to Bentham*, 157, George G Harrap & Co Ltd, 1942.
5. Cassirer, Ernst., op. cit., 75.
6. Gordon, Peter and Lawton, Denis, *Curriculum Change in the Nineteenth and Twentieth Centuries*, 52, Hodder and Stoughton, 1978.
7. Rousseau, Jean-Jacques. *The Essential Rousseau*, 81, translated by Lowell Blair, Mentor, New American Library, New York, 1974.
8. Gordon, Peter and Lawton, Denis, op. cit., 52 and Rousseau, Jean-Jacques, *Emile*, op.cit., 123, 125.
9. Ibid.
10. Jimack, P D. Introduction, xv, in op. cit., *Emile*.
11. Ibid., ix.
12. Rousseau, Jean-Jacques. Foxley Barbara translated, op. cit., 111.
13. Leonard, Fred Eugene, AM, MD, *A Guide to the History of Physical Education*, 1947, 67, 68, Greenwood Press, Connecticut, Third Edition Revised & Enlarged, 1971.
14. Ibid.,

15. Ibid., 69.
16. Stewart, W A C, *Progressive and Radicals in English Education 1750-1970*, 15, MacMillan, 1972.
17. Leonard, Fred Eugene, op. cit., 70
18. Ibid., 71.
19. GutsMuths, J C F, *Gymnastics for Youth*, after the end pages, Printed for J. Johnson, 1800.
20. Ibid., e.g., 131, 145.
21. Ibid., e.g., 20.
22. Ibid., e.g., 22.
23. Ibid., e.g. 130.
24. Galen, *Selected Works, To Thrasyboulos: is healthiness a part of medicine or gymnastics?* Translated with an Introduction and Notes by Singer P N, The World's Classics, Oxford University Press, 1997.
25. Tissot, Joseph-Clement, *Medicinal and Surgical Gymnastics*, 1780, Bastien, Little Lion Street, Paris. Licht, Elizabeth, New Haven, Connecticut, 1964.
26. Ibid., preface, v-vii.
27. Ibid., 6.
28. GutsMuths, J C F, op. cit., 27.
29. Montesquieu, Baron de, *The Spirit of the Laws*, 1748, Book XIV, 212-35, Book XIX, 292-395, Hafner Press, New York, 1949.
30. GutsMuths, J C F, op. cit., viii.
31. Mallon, Bill and Buchanan, Ian, *The Olympic Games: Results for All Competitors and All Events with Commentary*, 115, Mc Farland, North Carolina, 2000, Scarecrow Press, Inc., Lanham, USA.
32. McIntosh, P C, *Physical Education in England since 1800*, 12, Bell and Hyman, 1968.
33. Ibid., 98
34. Ibid., 113.
35. PP Volume XLIII, 1861, *Royal Commission to Enquire into the Present State of Popular Education in England, and to consider and Report what measures, if any, are required for the extension of Sound and Cheap Elementary Instruction to all classes of the People.*
36. Frow, Edmund and Ruth, *A Survey of the Half-time System in Education*, 17, E J Morton, Didsbury, Manchester, 1970.
37. PP. XLIII, 1862, Accounts and Papers, *Copy of Two Papers submitted to the (Newcastle) Commission by Mr Chadwick*, one entitled Communications on Half-Time Teaching and on military drills, the other a letter to Mr Senior explanatory of the former paper. Printed 21 March 1862. First letter 69 pages. Second letter 69 pages.
38. PP Volume XLIII, 1861, op. cit., 66.
39. Ibid., 67.
40. Ibid.
41. Collins, Phillip, *Dickens and Educaton*, 82, MacMillan & Co. Ltd., 1963.
42. Ibid., 236.
43. Ibid., 81.
44. Ibid.
45. Ibid., 225.
46. Ibid., 82.
47. Frow, Edmund and Ruth, op. cit., 25.
48. Ibid., 373.
49. *The Times*, 22 June 1870, 5.
50. Ibid.
51. Ibid., 14 September 1869, 7.
52. Floud, Roderick, Wachter, Kenneth and Gregory, Annabel. *Height, Health and History*, 224, CUP 1990.

53. Knolly, W W, Captain, 'Recruiting for the army' in *MacMillans Magazine*, No. 58 Volume X, MacMillan & Co., August 1864.
54. TNA WO/32/6209, Parkes E A, MD, FRS, Appendix A Memo by Dr Parkes, 4, in Hammersley, F, *et.al.*, *Report of the Committee appointed to Report upon Gymnastic Instruction for the Army*, 25 January 1864, 1-10.
55. Ibid., Appendix A, 4.
56. Ibid., 1, para 1.
57. Ibid., 1,para 2.
58. Ibid., Appendix B, 5.
59. Ibid., 1, para 2.
60. Floud, Roderick, *et al.*, op. cit., 57.
61. Ibid.
62. Ibid.
63. Ibid.

APPENDIX III
OVERPRESSURE

The concept of overpressure was investigated by James Crichton-Browne MD (1840-1938) at the invitation of Anthony John Mundella (1825-1897), Vice-President of the Committee of the Council on Education (Education Department) in 1884.[1]

Crichton-Browne identified "examination fever" as the bane of the elementary schoolchild.[2] Examinations, he declared, instead of being tests on school work had become, to a great extent, its one aim and guiding principle. According to Crichton-Browne overpressure acted most severely on backward children which he classified into three groups: the dull, the starved and the delicate. He also identified starvation as the most important question facing elementary schools in London.[3]

Conversations held by Crichton-Browne with children in the course of his enquiry revealed that between 6% and 9% of children whom he interviewed on any one day had no breakfast.[4] Several reasons were given to Crichton-Browne by the children for this state of affairs: father unemployed, father in hospital, no bread in the house or the mother still apparently under the influence of the previous night's drinking.[5] Equally, many other children were half-starved not through lack of food but through non-nutritious sustenance. It was necessary, therefore, that liberal and regular feeding should take place in order that a child should be prepared "to profit by education".[6]

In a memorandum[7], replying to Dr Crichton-Browne's report, Joseph Girling Fitch (1824-1903), HMI, who accompanied Crichton-Browne on his visits to schools in Lambeth, upon which Crichton-Browne's report was based, criticised the basis, i.e. Substance of the report.[8] In doing so he expressed the

> "well-known physiological truth that intellectual effort is not only helpful but almost essential to physical well-being."[9]

The logic of this argument was carried forward by Fitch as the hope that:

> " statesmen and philanthropists........will think twice before........mixing up (national education)......with the administration of food and medicine to the children of the poor......the enforcement of any human duty as a legal duty weakens the essence of a moral obligation."[10]

The provision of free dinners, for example, determined many idle and improvident parents to neglect their children, send them to school badly clothed and miserable, in the hope that the children would attract sympathy and encourage others to feed children at other people's expense.

Fitch was certain that if the State or any other public body began to provide food or other medical assistance for all the children in the elementary schools that required it, there would be a large number of parents whose diminished sense of responsibility might become a serious public danger.[11]

Notes

1. PP. 61, 1884, 293, *Report of Dr Crichton-Browne on Overpressure*, 1-54.
2. Ibid., 7.
3. Ibid., 8
4. Ibid., 8-9.
5. Ibid., 9.
6. Ibid., 10.
7. PP. 61, 1884, 293, 55-79, *Memorandum relating to Dr Crichton-Browne's Report* by Mr J G Fitch, one of Her Majesty's Chief Inspectors of Schools.
8. Ibid., 78-9.
9. Ibid., 59.
10. Ibid., 77.
11. Ibid.

APPENDIX IV
THE CONCEPT OF PHYSICAL DETERIORATION-1

The concept of physical deterioration/degeneration was to exert a significant and profound impact upon the minds of the governing classes up to and beyond the passing of the 1906 Act. In the investigations that lead to the 1903 and 1904 Reports, the conclusions reiterated the nature of poverty and social deprivation and were at the heart of the perceived physical deterioration in the urban working classes and their children in the elementary schools.

Karl Popper (1902-1994) considered that Plato's (c427-347BC) concept of political degeneration depended mainly on moral degeneration, which, in turn, was due to racial degeneration.[1] This was the way in which the general cosmic law of decay manifested itself in human affairs.[2] Referring to *The Laws* (350-340BC),[3] the lessons of history suggested that the State, which was free of the evil and corruption of change, was the most perfect kind of State.[4] Plato's *Theory of Forms* may thus be interpreted as a reaction to the decay of contemporary events.[5] Necessity thus demanded that historical decay and deterioration were eliminated and the way that that was to be done was in the notion of the arrested State.[6] Although Plato accepted the decline of the social order in all societies, what he appears to have postulated was that historical decline was a linear affair, from one type of constitutional government to the next without any prospect of arresting the decline through any kind of social intervention.[7]

In England, William Farr (1807-1883), compiler of statistics for the Registrar-General (RGO),[8] used the expressions *public medicine* or *public health medicine* emphasizing that public health had a medical aspect to it and that medicine had a responsibility for the *Public Health*.[9]

Farr was one of those social reformers who believed that environmental factors contributed to the spread of disease and, therefore, in order to prevent disease, the environment that caused it, should be destroyed.[10] There was a sense, therefore, that the environment could be healthily reclaimed by destruction. There was a similar sense in which Farr's vision of the poor as wretched, but redeemable creatures, prevailed through an examination of urban mortality through the use of statistics. On this analysis he was able to construct reform on the basis that high mortality was caused by urban overcrowding.[11]

Nevertheless, Farr recognised that different members of different families appeared to suffer from different diseases even within the same environment.[12] He concluded that people were predisposed to hereditary conditions of disease and that this predisposition extended to the world's different races.[13]

During the last few years of his career Farr was chairman of the Anthropometric Committee of the British Association.[14] The committee collected information on age, sex, race, height, weight, hair colour, girth of chest, strength of arm and eyesight mainly of British soldiers, students and civil servants.[15] The reason why anthropometry became so important in the late 19th century was the fear that racial degeneration would occur in unhealthy environments.[16] Although Farr lacked facts in his assessment of environmentally induced degeneration, he was certain of its validity.[17] Children who lived in high density urban districts with high mortality rates were liable to weakness or disablement.[18] Farr, thus, postulated a health policy which averted sickness and death by increasing

> "........the energy of all vital forces whether nutritive, formative, locomotive or sensitive and intellectual."[19]

This statement was made in his first published article made ten years earlier in 1835.[20] Nevertheless, the weak and disabled not affected by environmental hostility would still live and pass on their genes to their offspring.[21] The Spartans had evolved one solution to this dilemma[22] but it was one that was now clearly untenable. So how could mankind be raised to divine perfection? The answer was that human reproduction should be controlled for social ends.[23] Soldiers ought to be encouraged to marry in order to transmit *valour*. There were dangers to the race in the freedom of criminals, the insane and people with hereditary diseases to reproduce.[24] Whereas (Sir) Francis Galton (1822-1911) was later to advocate marriage and reproduction as socially desirable, Farr's ideas led him to the notion that the unfit should be prohibited from reproduction.[25]

Foucault has noted that an analysis of hereditary conditions was putting sex – sexual relations, venereal diseases, matrimonial alliances and perversions – into a consideration of *biological responsibility* by the human species since sex could not only be affected by its own diseases, but could, if not controlled transmit diseases or create others, which might affect future generations. Consequently, not only was medical management necessary in a State but also the political construction of organizing the State's management of births, marriages and deaths.[26]

Another perspective on physical deterioration in the late 19th century was that of asylum.[27] Moral therapeutic treatment, designed to meet a variety of mental disorders[28], failed to have an effect, especially on those whose conduct and behaviour was apparently aberrant rather than congenital.[29] So all kinds of aberration and disorder indicated that insanity was organic and passed on from generation to generation.[30] Thus, there was little chance of remedial action. The asylum was, therefore, the only placement for those unfortunates assigned there, where they would be unable to pass on their degenerate genes.[31] One of these degenerist psychiatric doctors in England was Henry Maudsley MD (1835-1918).[32] He explained[33] degeneracy in the following terms.

Survival of the fittest did not necessarily mean the survival of the highest organism.[34] It meant only the survival of that which was best suited to the circumstances, good or bad. A decline from a higher to a lower level of being, the process of degeneration, was integral to the economy of nature.[35] Each individual, each family and each nation might take either an upward course of evolution or a downward course of degeneracy.[36]

What degeneracy meant was *unkinding*, the undoing of a *kind*. Originally, he noted, this term was neutral in so far as it could be understood as both evolutionary and degenerate, but was now[37] used exclusively to denote the change from a higher to a lower state. It was a process of *dissolution* rather than its opposite *involution*, the state prior to evolution.[38]

Degeneration was, in fact, a transformation from one form of *kind* to a new or abnormal *kind* but a *kind* incapable of rising in the scale of development[39] with a natural tendency to sink lower on lower.[40] This manifested itself in the individual in three stages:

(a) an absence of exercise which produced social, moral and volitional decay in one generation

(b) the mental derangement or such a development of vice in the character of the succeeding generation which falls only a little short of madness or crime
(c) while in the third generation there followed moral imbecility or idiocy with or without corresponding intellectual infirmity.[41]

The concept of a degenerative pathology was exemplified in the notion of *Fin de siècle*, a French phrase meaning the end of the century, referenced, in historical terms, to the final decades of the 19th century.[42] However, its general application embraced ideas of symbolism and decadence in various worlds of science, psychology, politics, social, sexual and artistic expression. Interpretatively, its rationale was that of an apocalyptic vision of the end of civilisation, which, in actuality, did not achieve its end until the beginning of the First World War.[43]

The origin of these ideas of an inherited and transmitted pathology was the French school of Psychiatry. Benedict Augustin Morel (1809-1873) intellectualized degeneration as a morbid deviation from a perfect primitive type. Moreover, deviation was subject to the *law of progressivity* compounding deviation through the generations.[44]

Morel's analysis highlighted three categories of the symptoms responsible for the disease: (a) physical deformity; (b) perversion of the organism; (c) the disturbance of the emotional faculties.[45]

Morel's conception was coherently relevant to ideas associated with Jean Baptiste Lamarck (1744-1829), since changes in hereditary were relative to the effort of an organism to adapt to the changed circumstances of environmental conditions. Consequently, it was possible to deductively assert that if social behaviour followed the laws of natural selection, then, the transmission of social characteristics were just as much probable as those of the physiological.[46]

Nevertheless, the identification of the degenerate was exemplified by Max Nordau (1849-1923) as tormented by doubt, seeking the basis of all phenomena, especially those whose first causes were completely inaccessible to us and was unhappy when his enquiries and ruminations led to no result.[47] As a result the degenerate was incapable of adaptation to existing circumstances and, was, basically, an example of a delirious manifestation of mysticism exhibited through an excessive development of the powers of imagination.[48] Nevertheless, this aspect of deterioration/degeneration found its focus in the world of art and literature.[49]

This aspect of the degeneration/deterioration synthesis was related, but not immediately pertinent, to the urban conditions of the working classes, which arose through the enormous span of social and industrial change during the nineteenth century.[50] In terms of the eighteenth century, where a more settled cycle of nature prevailed, these changes were prodigious in scope.[51] Those 19th-century conditions caused the governing classes to redefine the terms of the Public Health in the light of new medical and environmental insights into the physiological conditions of the working classes in their existential habitats.

Notes

1. Popper, Karl. *The Open Society and Its Enemies, The Spell of Plato*, Volume 1, 20. Routledge & Kegan Paul, London 1945.
2. Ibid.

3. Plato. *The Laws*, (350 BC), Book 3, 118-56. Saunders, Trevor J, translated, Penguin, Harmondsworth, 1970.
4. Popper, Karl, op. cit., 21
5. Lee H D P, translated. Introduction, 9-11, in Plato, *The Republic*, (380 BC), 9-404, Penguin Classics, Harmondsworth, 1955.
6. Ibid., 21, see also Popper, Karl, op. cit., (notes 208-310).
7. Plato. *The Republic*, op.cit. para 546, 315; *see also* Cross, R C and Woozley, A D, Plato's *Republic*, 262, Macmillan, St Martin's Press, London 1964.
8. Hodgkinson, Ruth G. *The Origins of the National Health Service, The Medical Services of the New Poor Law, 1834-1871*, 26, The Wellcome Historical Medical Library, 1967.
9. Fee, Elizabeth and Acheson Roy, Eds, *A History of Education in Public Health*, 9, Oxford University Press, 1991.
10. Porter, Dorothy, *Health, Civilization and the State*, 72, Routledge, London 1999.
11. Ibid.
12. Eyler, John M. *Victorian Social Medicine*, 154, John Hopkins University Press, Baltimore, 1979.
13. Ibid.
14. Ibid., 155.
15. Ibid.
16. Ibid.
17. Ibid., 155-6.
18. Ibid., 156.
19. Ibid.
20. Ibid.
21. Ibid., 157.
22. Ibid.
23. Ibid.
24. Ibid., 158.
25. Ibid.
26. Foucault, Michel, *The History of Sexuality*, 24-26, Penguin Books, Harmondsworth, 1987.
27. Porter, Roy, Madness and its Institutions, 277-302, in Wear, Andrew, Editor, *Medicine In Society*, 298-9, CUP, 1992.
28. Ibid., 298.
29. Ibid., 299.
30. Ibid.
31. Ibid., 300.
32. Ibid., 299.
33. Maudsley, Henry. *Body and Will*, 237, Kegan Paul, Trench & Co, London, 1883.
34. Ibid.
35. Ibid.,
36. Ibid., 238.
37. Ibid., 240.
38. Ibid.
39. Ibid., 241.
40. Ibid.
41. Ibid., 248.
42. Ledger, Sally and Luckhurst, Roger, Editors, *The Fin De Siecle, A Reader in Cultural History, c. 1880-1900*, 1-363, OUP, 2000.
43. Ensor, Robert. *England 1870-1914*, 540-57, Oxford, Clarendon Press, 1968.
44. Greenslade, William. *Degeneration, Culture and the Novel 1880-1940*, 16, CUP, 1994.
45. Ibid.
46. Ibid., 17.
47. Nordau, Max Simon. *Degeneration*, (1895), 17, General Books, Danvers, Massachusetts, 2009.

48. Ibid., 19.
49. Greenslade, William, op. cit., 1-355.
50. Jordan, Thomas E. *The Degeneracy Crisis and Victorian Youth*, 24, State University of New York Press, Albany, New York, USA, 1993.
51. Ibid.

APPENDIX V
DEGENERATION FROM THE BOER WAR TO 1905

The end of the Boer War on the 24 March 1902 coincided with the introduction of the Education Bill into the House of Commons[1] by the Prime Minister, Arthur James Balfour (1848-1930), First Earl of Balfour. It was read a second time on 8 May 1902 and passed its third reading on 3 December 1902. Sent to the House of Lords on the same day when it was read a first time, read a second time on the 5 December 1902 and a third time on the 15 December 1902; receiving the Royal Assent on the 18 December 1902.[2]

J C Colvill, Surrey HMI, disclosed in his evidence on 24 April 1901 in the *Departmental Committee on Training College Courses of Instruction* (1901) (supra chapter 1) that a Model Course (supra chapter 1) was in course of preparation by the Board. The final proof was to be settled on Saturday 27 April 1901. The course covered the first part of the Army Drill Book, including all the physical training, physical exercises, free gymnastics and dumb-bell work. One of the principles underlying the Model Course was to implement a national system because under the then present conditions

> "a man comes into London and he learns Chesterton's system ; he goes to Liverpool and he must follow Alexander's system, or in Birmingham or Leicester, Bott's or Oxley's system, and elsewhere yet other systems."[3]

Moreover, there was a case for girls as well as boys to do military drill,[4] *since modern military drill had as much to recommend it as Swedish drill*[5] (author's italics).

The Model Course came under much criticism,[6] was eventually replaced by the 1904 Syllabus (supra chapter 1), which had two purposes; the physical effect and the educational effect. The former was to improve the health and physique of the children, the latter, the development of the scholars' qualities of alertness, decision, concentration and perfect control of mind over body.[7]

This general transition was, to some extent, the result of two articles by Major-General Sir Frederick Maurice (1841-1912) in *The Contemporary Review*.[8] Maurice had pointed out in the first of these articles that teeth were the problem of many recruits whose problems were exacerbated by the fact that they did not receive proper nutrition during the period of childhood.[9]

The crux of the matter was, however, the inadequate development in health of the youth of the country. Maurice asked the question:

> "Should we not regard education, as the Romans did, as the means of providing a sound mind in a sound body?[10]

Mothers were largely to blame. The food they provided for their children was appalling.[11] The gymnasium, the training of mothers in the provision of food knowledge and MI was required, all of which should be subject to constant supervision by medical experts, a development that would be classified as education.[12] The conjunction of education with the housing problem, the problem of milk in the early years and the curse of early marriages needed to be addressed.[13]

In the second article, Maurice modified his views of mothers' abilities to provide wholesome food for their children citing the work of Rowntree in that the conditions of modern life did not allow them to supply their children with sufficient food.[14] What was the truth? Investigation could clarify the real meaning of the army recruiting statistics of 5:2, i.e. out of every five men who wished to enlist and primarily offered themselves for enlistment, there were only two recruits out of every five remaining in the army after two years.[15]

On 31 January 1903, *The Lancet* published a leading article entitled *An Impeachment of the National Health*,[16] which referred specifically to the second of Maurice's articles in *The Contemporary Review*. In one respect, that leader, was a condemnation of the procedures adopted by the army of their recruiting procedures which only accepted two out of every five men after two years of military service.[17]

Nevertheless, *The Lancet* leader questioned the legitimacy of Maurice's statistics and general conclusions. All the statistics of Public Health suggested, it argued, that the efforts of preventative medicine and the spread of education had immensely bettered the general health of the nation. Nonetheless, there was a large quantity of the "shiftless class" who had been badly fed, badly housed, had had their confidence dashed by failure and had consistently and regularly failed to take common sanitary precautions. It was the town populations that were the exemplars of this state of affairs.[18]

In a letter to *The Lancet* 14 February 1903, Lauder Brunton referred to Maurice's second article and to *The Lancet*'s leader. Brunton refers to the two out of five statistics as an appalling fact.[19] However, he wonders what can be done for the children caught up in this statistic and calls for information regarding "physical deficiency"; the best means of remedying the defects and the best means currently available in case the best means possible cannot as yet be applied.[20] What this seems to have meant was that early marriages were a problem for leisure activity and that the problem might be solved for men

> "........by developing their interest in volunteering through regular training at school in the use of the rifle between the ages of seven and fourteen years......The success-obtained by Colonel Fox in the development of young recruits by physical exercises .....while their training in the use of the rifle would enable them to learn all the necessary drill much more quickly than at present........"[21]

He went on to say that the wonders achieved in the Russian army were both moral and provided a wonderful training in industrial skills.[22]

In parliament, concern was expressed on army enlistment:

> "the one subject which created anxiety at the present moment was the deterioration of the physique of recruits"[23]

Speaking during the debate, John Burns MP (1858-1943) noted that the subject that caused most concern was the paragraph of the Report of the Inspector-General of Recruiting 1902, which referred to the gradual deterioration of the physique of the working classes from which the bulk of recruits were drawn.[24]

The motion, which sought to ensure the character of the recruit on enlistment,[25] would be of little importance so long as industrial conditions remained as they were.[26] The motion would not be a substitute for badly-cooked food, for tinned food and adulterated food. It was no substitute for the lack of milk and good bread for children or for excessive labour during their period of growth.[27] Early marriages and intermittent employment would not solve the problem of the moral wrecks and physical wastrels who called on the recruiting sergeant.[28] In the end the motion resolved:

> "that......in order to adequately fit the British soldier for his duties at home and abroad, greater efforts should be made and precautions taken to secure an adequate standard of physique of recruits accepted....."[29]

In the Lords, Lord Meath rose to draw attention of the government to the 1903 Report and the Report of the Inspector-General of Recruiting to which Burns had referred. The 1903 Report postulated an undeniable degeneration of individuals of the classes where food and environment were defective, which called for attention and amelioration in obvious ways, one of which was a well-regulated system of PT.[30]

Quoting Lord Beaconsfield, Meath noted that Public Health was the foundation on which reposed the happiness of the people and the power of a country. Public Health was the first duty of a Statesman.[31] Meath, was, in fact, regurgitating in a different form the Roman aphorism: *Salus populi suprema lex – the public safety is the supreme law*,[32] a dictum that had been echoed by Thomas Hill Green (1878-1882), Whyte's Professor of Moral Philosophy concerning the consumption of drink.[33] The present situation was antagonistic to the public health of children. Children had to have strong and healthy parents, good and ample food, plenty of fresh air and exercise, be properly housed and have lead regular, disciplined lives. He quoted Burns MP:

> "The conditions essential to manhood begin before the body is born – a healthy home, reasonable labour, temperate living on the part of a father and mother, these are indispensible preliminaries to the healthy life of children. Fathers must drink less beer and mothers less tea."[34]

The principle requisites of a healthy and physical population were:
(a) healthy parents
(b) sanitary homes
(c) good abundant and well-cooked food including a cheap supply of fresh milk
(d) pure air and water
(e) facilities for exercise and healthy recreation
(f) a good educational system which shall combine physical with mental and moral training and shall instruct the young especially the girls in the elements of hygiene, dietetics, the care of infants and home sanitation, bringing them up under good and healthy moral surroundings.[35]

On Tuesday 21 July 1903, a dinner, held at the Athenaeum Club, at which Maurice was but one of the speakers, proposed the formation of *A National Physical Education League*.[36] The report of the dinner by John Black Atkins, editor of *The Manchester Guardian*, which had run a series of articles on PT and which were later published in *National Physical Training, An Open Debate* (1904) (supra Chapter 1) and had been antagonistic to the *Model Course*. During the debate following the dinner the view was expressed:

> ".....that proper feeding is not merely the necessary precedent to proper physical exercise, but that proper physical exercise is the necessary precedent to the proper assimilation of food in the body"[37]

The scheme, which was subsequently outlined and less than enthusiastically supported by Atkins, was proposed as *The Physical Improvement League* but was virtuously extolled by Lauder Brunton.[38]

In December 1903, the *British Medical Journal* (BMJ) published a series of articles on Physical Degeneration, the third of which concentrated on:

(a)   The Health of Mothers
(b)   Overlaying
(c)   The First Two Years
(d)   Milk
(e)   The Diet of the Poorer Classes

The latter[39] suggested that little attention was paid to the feeding of growing children and it quoted from a study of the diets of the labouring classes, noting that since food was the sole source of energy required for (a) building up the body, (b) doing work, (c) maintaining the temperature, it was obvious that the working capacity and well-being of a community was largely influenced by the food supply eaten by each individual. Without this, growth and development was impossible, working capacity diminished and a predisposition to disease was induced.[40]

Basically, the poor ate food which was in line with the money in their pockets so that the average person selected the different foods in the market with less knowledge of their actual value – as a source of nourishment – than was found in almost any other line of purchases.[41]

On Wednesday 28 June 1905 the *National League for Physical Education and Improvement* was inaugurated at a meeting at the Mansion House.[42] The chairman of the meeting was James Crichton-Browne (1840-1938), the author of the 1884 Report on *Overpressure*.[43] Not only was the meeting attended by many prominent people, the speech of Richard Burdon Haldane (1856-1928), Liberal Imperialist, and Secretary of State for War (December 1905-1912) noted:

> "…….education is a far bigger thing than mere learning….it means…attention to the physical conditions of life …….you cannot save the soul unless you attend to the body…….it is not to be wondered at that Parliament (has been discussing the)….feeding of children in schools"[44]

This statement echoes an article[45] by (Sir) Winston Churchill MP (1874-1965) published in the *Manchester Guardian* in 1903 suggesting that a Liberal Party consensus on the value of feeding children in the PES had been reached. Quoting Rowntree's studies Churchill asked:

> "Before you put these children to exercises of such a nature as would develop muscle, they must be fed…..The moment the State makes itself responsible for a compulsory system of physical training, it also makes itself responsible for seeing that those who have to undergo the training are in a fit condition to receive it"[46]

And this begged several other questions. Do you feed these children at the cost of the State or do you force the parents to feed them? Good food was the foundation of any system of PT and was prior to any decisions on the system of physical exercise or any system of military drill that might induce a military spirit and encourage recruitment for the army. Food was the most important factor in producing a healthy physique. If it were to be suggested that weak underfed children should be exempted from PT, then you would be neglecting the very children who most required care.⁴⁷

Concepts of physical deterioration/degeneration in the late 19th and early 20th centuries were inextricably linked with notions of various forms of physical exercise, including military drill, as the means by which this deterioration would be resolved. Gradually, however, it became clearer that differentiated social conditions were significant factors in the extent to which these conditions existed.

The 1903 and 1904 Reports clarified the situation but the appointment of yet another committee, whose 1905 Report (supra chapter 1) suggested that in spite of a wider and broader appreciation of the problem of physical deterioration/degeneration, and how it might be resolved, prevarication for one reason or another, prevailed.

The problem facing the government of the time, therefore, was this – was the democratic State a form of a Platonic "arrested" State preferring a physical state among its inhabitants of physical deterioration/degeneration, which would end in the ignominy of its own deterioration and the possible collapse of Empire (in the light of German expansionism) or was it to respect its citizenry by emboldening those citizens in the realization of their educational capacities and potentialities in accord with a developing liberal agenda, enunciated, among others, by Thomas Hill Green?*

---

*Between 1867 and 1874 Green had become a member of every Temperance Society in Oxford. He was Vice-president of the United Kingdom Alliance and became president of the Band of Hope Temperance Union (Greengarten page 91).

Notes

1. McIntosh, Peter C. *Physical Education in England Since 1800*, 143, Bell & Hyman, Revised & Enlarged Edition, London, 1968.
2. Drury, J F W. *Drury's Manual of Education*, 161-166, John Heywood, Manchester, 1903.
3. Education Department, *Memorandum of the Departmental Committee on Training College Courses of Instruction*, 1901, Minutes of Evidence 4606, 184.
4. Ibid., Minute 4610.
5. Ibid., Minute 4650.
6. McIntosh, Peter C, op. cit., 150.
7. Board of Education, *Syllabus of Physical Exercises for use in Public ElementarySchools*, 1904, 9.
8. Maurice, Major-General Sir Frederick (pseudonym Miles). 'Where To Get Men, 1902', 78-86, in *The Contemporary Review*, Volume LXXXI, January 1902; Maurice, Major-General Sir Frederick. 'National Health: A Soldier's Study, 1903', 41-56, in *The Contemporary Review*, Volume LXXXIII, January 1903; *see also* Penn, Alan, *Targeting Schools*, 111-113, Woburn Press, London, 1999.
9. Ibid., January 1902, 80.
10. Ibid., 85.
11. Ibid.,
12. Ibid.,
13. Ibid., January 1903, 44-6.
14. Ibid., 47.
15. Ibid., 56.
16. *The Lancet*, 31 Janury 1903, 315.

17. Ibid.
18. Ibid., 315-317.
19. Ibid., 14 February 1903, 471.
20. Ibid.
21. Ibid., 472.
22. Ibid.
23. *Hansard*, House of Commons, Fourth Series, Volume CXX, 25 March 1903, column 246.
24. Ibid., column 267.
25. Ibid.
26. Ibid.
27. Ibid.
28. Ibid., 268.
29. Ibid., 276.
30. *Hansard*, House of Lords, Fourth Series, Volume CXXIV, 6 July 1903, column 1324.
31. Ibid., column 1325.
32. Cicero. Keyes. *De Legibus*, translated by Clinton Walker, 52 BC, Book III, paragraphs 8-9, 467, Loeb Classical Library No. 213, Wm. Heinnemann, London, 1928.
33. *The Oxford Chronicle*, 4 February 1882, 6.
34. *Hansard*, House of Lords Debates, op. cit., Volume CXXIV, column 1330.
35. Ibid., column 1336.
36. *The Manchester Guardian*, 23 July 1903, 12, column 4.
37. Ibid.
38. Brunton, Lauder, 'Progress of Proposed National League For Physical Education and Improvement' in Brunton, Lauder, Sir, *Collected Papers on Physical and Military Training*, 1-12, London, Publisher Not Stated, 1915.
39. BMJ, 5 December 1903, 1472-1474.
40. Ibid., 1472.
41. Ibid.
42. Reported by a member of *The Times* Staff, National League For Physical Education And Improvement (The Inaugural Meeting of the League Wednesday, 28 June 1905 at the Mansion House), 1-24, in Brunton, Lauder, Sir, *Collected Papers*, op. cit., 1.
43. PP. 61, 1884, 293, *Report of Dr Crichton-Browne on Overpressure*, 1-53.
44. Brunton, Lauder, 'National League For Physical Education And Improvement' (28 June 1905), 15-16, in Brunton, Lauder, Sir, *Collected Papers*, op. cit.
45. Atkins, John Black, *National Physical Training, An Open Debate*, 70-3, Isbister & Co, 1904.
46. Ibid., 71
47. Ibid., 71-72.

APPENDIX VI
DEGENERATION-EUGENICS

The eugenics movement originated in England and was a product of Social Darwinism, a theory influential in the 19th-century, which argued that societies, as with species, were subject to the laws of natural selection as theorised by Charles Darwin (1809-1882) in *On The Origin of Species By Means of Natural Selection* (1859).

Francis Galton (1822-1911) coined the term eugenics to introduce the science of improving the quality of the human race. Those people that tended to the betterment of the species were eugenic. Those that made the race less strong were dysgenic.

The latter, thought Galton, should be discouraged from reproducing since the appearance was that the poorer classes seemed to turn the notion of an upward and onward evolution of the human race on its head as the poorest classes were the most fertile and fit.

In taking this approach, he was at odds with Darwin's view that natural selection acted only in a tentative manner. In certain circumstances, Darwin observed, individuals and races could have built up certain self-evident advantages, but, on the other hand, failed to build up other features characteristic of the whole.[1]

In spite of these different interpretations, Galton set up eugenic societies, a eugenics laboratory and a Research Fellowship at University College in 1907 and a journal devoted to the subject.

Galton founded eugenics with the aim of raising the physical and mental level of the race with two ideas as the basis of its rationale:

(a) desirable physical and mental qualities were unevenly distributed throughout the population, and, therefore,
(b) those who had the desirable qualities should be identified and encouraged to multiply faster than the others.

The logic of this position was that the identification of desirable qualities for the purposes of reproduction was much more that of social administration, and, consequently was less than hostile to certain forms of government intervention. Indeed, the participation of certain political heavyweights in the eugenics movement, such as Arthur James Balfour (1848-1930), who, as Prime Minister, had personally introduced the 1902 Act on the 24 May 1902 in to the House of Commons, suggests that their motivation was more that of social administration than that of a more sinister involvement than has been suggested. A similar observation may be made about William Henry Beveridge (1879-1963),[2] although that should be considered in the light of remarks he had made concerning the unemployed.[3]

The contextual difference between the eugenicist and the social reformer was that the former accepted a fixed conservative component of human nature whereas the social reformer placed a reliance on social policy.

In some respects, it is possible to articulate the nature of eugenics as a problem of equality. In Genesis, for example, male and female were created in God's image.[4] While the capacities of individuals varied, it was, as T H Green observed, necessary to develop educational opportunities in order to create a citizenry of equals.[5]

Notes

1. Jones, Greta. *Social Darwinism and English Thought, The Interaction between Biological and Social Theory*, 99-100, The Harvester Press Limited, Brighton, Sussex, England, 1980.
2. Sewell, Dennis. *The Political Gene, How Darwin's Ideas Changed Politics*, 55-77, Picador, London, 2009.
3. Heater, Derek. *Citizenship: The Civic Ideal in World History, Politics and Education*, 76, Longman, London, 1990.
4. Genesis, *The Holy Bible*, Chapter 1, verse 27.
5. Richter, Melvin, *The Politics of Conscience*, T H Green and His Age, 354, University Press of America, Lanham, New York, 1983. 1st. published 1964.

It should be noted that:
Aldrich, Richard and Gordon, Peter, *Dictionary of British Educationists*, 92, Woburn Press, London, 1989 present a resume of Galton's life.

And information and interpretations in:
Freeden, Michael, *Liberal Languages*, 146 etcetera, Princeton University Press, Princeton, New Jersey, 2005.
Richards, Janet Radcliffe, *Human Nature after Darwin, A Philosophical Introduction*, 221-222, Routledge, 2000.
Searle, G R, *The Quest for National Efficiency, A Study of British Politics and Political Thought, 1899-1914*, 61-62, Basil Blackwell, Oxford, 1971.

APPENDIX VII
SIR GEORGE MALCOLM FOX

Colonel Sir George Malcolm Fox died aged 75 years on 10 March 1918 at Rustington House, Rustington, Sussex. He was born in 1843 the son of Mr. Douglas Fox, a surgeon, living at 98 Friar Gate, Derby when the young Fox was eight years of age. His mother was Marianne Fox, then thirty-seven years old. He was awarded his knighthood in 1910.

In 1861 the family was living at 135 Marine Parade, Brighton. His father was then aged sixty-three and registered as a magistrate and not practicing medical surgery. His wife was then aged forty-seven and the 1861 census records show that there were five other siblings consisting of one brother and four sisters.

Fox was married on 8 September 1881 at Sandown, Isle of Wight to Mary Rose "Minnie" Newall, who had been born on 30 November 1859 in India. She died in Glasgow on 11 July 1882. They had one child Mary Agnes Dorothy Fox born on 6 July 1882 in North Breton, Glasgow.

He married his second wife Marion June Mills on 28 July 1884. Her address was The Gymnasium, Aldershot.

Fox entered the army as an Ensign (2nd lieutenant) by purchase on 22 December 1863. After several transfers between the Regiments of Foot, he was promoted to lieutenant on 9 June 1865 and to captain in the 100th Regiment of Foot on 10 June 1871.

In November 1873, Fox refereed a boxing match at the back of a public house, "The Fountain", Penny Street, Portsmouth. The match was between James Lynch, aged twenty-two, a dockyard worker, and George Baker, a professional boxer. As a result of injuries sustained during the fight, Lynch died. Consequently, several of the organizing and participating officials were arrested and charged with manslaughter, Fox being among them. The trial date was fixed for 11 December 1873. Subsequently, the jury dismissed the charges against all concerned on the direction of the judge at Winchester Crown Court.[1]

In 1875 Fox joined the 42nd Regiment of Foot, the Black Watch, part of the Royal Highlanders Brigade.

In 1882 Fox was in Egypt with the Black Watch where he captured a sword[2] from Arabi Pasha's tent even though he was injured during the battle of Tel-el-Kebir.[3] An account of the political history of Britain's involvement in Egypt at this time may be found in *England 1810-1914*, 1936.[4]

The Black Watch had been sent to Egypt to protect the economic interests of European Governments. Britain's interests, in particular, were centred around the Suez Canal, which was of important strategic interest in regard to access to India.

When the Egyptians revolted against the interference of the European Powers, the Black Watch was dispatched as part of the Highland Brigade, which also included the Gordon and Cameron Highlanders and the Highland Light Infantry. The Brigade headed for Tel-el-Kabir, strategically placed between the Suez Canal, Alexandria and Cairo. Arabi Pashi, controlled

20,000 men at Tel-el-Kabir, situated in flat desert terrain, and difficult to approach without giving away their imminent arrival. So, after marching through the night and arriving at sunrise, they caught the Egyptians off-guard. The Highland Brigade put them to flight on 13 September 1882.

On 23 July 1883 Fox was promoted Major and appointed as Deputy-Assistant-Adjutant and Quarter Master General to perform the duties of Assistant Inspector of the Army Gymnasium at Aldershot. Promoted to Lieutenant Colonel on 25 July 1888, he was made full Colonel on 21 April 1889, at which point, he was promoted to Inspector.

Few civilians and even fewer soldiers in high places realized what Malcolm Fox did in making the men efficient in the use of their weapons in personal combat. The majority of British soldiers had the instinct for hand-to-hand fighting but their success was materially helped by the lessons learned in the gymnasium.

Colonel Fox, as Assistant Inspector of Gymnasia and in charge of the headquarters of the system at Aldershot, entirely altered the course of instruction.

The army instructors originally taught the method of instruction under the superintendence of Archibald Maclaren but were latterly allowed to drift away from the fight system, which was to promote general bodily improvement, and, by exercises, to instill confidence in hand-to-hand fighting.

Colonel Fox elaborated a system of attack and defence, inventing and patenting a new form of spring rifle, with which, a vigorous thrust could be made without risk of damage to an opponent. Later, he initiated bayonet-fighting competitions in battalions and companies, and inaugurated annual army bayonet competitions at the Royal Naval and Military Tournament.

He constructed the Army athletic training ground outside the Aldershot main gymnasium, entirely at his own expense. When he introduced boxing instruction, he hired two highly *competent* boxers and the result was the beginning and institution of boxing competitions in all army units and Public Schools.

The Duke of Connaught, at Colonel Fox's suggestion, gave a challenge shield for a cross-country obstacle race between teams of two officers and 100 other ranks of all units.

Subsequently, dissatisfied with the swordsmanship of officers, he visited all the best continental schools, finally deciding that the system taught by Signor Il Cavaliere Masiello was the best on offer.

He spent two months in that school at Florence, bringing to England Signor Magnini in April 1893, as an instructor, who was joined by Masiello himself in the following June. The two instructors took classes in succession from all units of the army and improved the art of swordsmanship beyond recognition.

Colonel Fox was, then, satisfied with progress in sword and bayonet but was also determined to institute an improved system of PT for recruits. Consequently, he went to Stockholm, accompanied by several Staff instructors. On his return, much impressed, he tried to introduce the army to the Swedish system of drill. He was turned down on the grounds that too much academic training was required for both officers and men. Nevertheless, a free gymnastics system was introduced, when in 1906 the Army introduced the Swedish system. From 1897-1900 he acted as Assistant Adjutant General of the North Eastern District HQ York.

Retiring under the age clause, he was employed by the Board of Education as HMI of PT. He also served as a member of the *Inter-Departmental Committee on Physical Deterioration*, and on the *Inter-Departmental Committee on the Model Course of Physical Exercises*, both of which reported in 1904. (supra chapter 1)

Chapter 2 (supra) relates the gathering at Aldershot of a demonstration of children at the army school there, which, in retrospect, seems to have been a concerted effort to develop a new course of physical exercises, which unfortunately seems to have resulted in the Model Course. The Army Schools, at that time, were not under the control of the Board of Education. Accordingly the standards of PT in the army schools was said to be aimed at the concept of a healthy body.[5] Moreover, this conceptual approach to PT was recollected as more in tune with the Danish system as Colonel Fox was said to believe that the Swedish system of drill emphasised the curative and aesthetic aspects of physical exercise.[6] If this were true, Fox's appointment at the Board may possibly have been based on the premise that the assumed physical deterioration of the British race required more than a curative and aesthetic response.

Notes

1. *The Hampshire Advertiser*, 12 November 1873, 22 November 1873 and *The Isle of Wight Observer*, 20 December 1873; TNA, HO 140/22 A Calendar of Prisoners Tried at at Assizes and Quarter Sessions, Winter Gaol Delivery.
2. A cartoon of Colonel Fox appears in *Vanity Fair*, 3 September 1896 entitled "Swordsmanship".
3. The Black Watch Castle Museum, Perth, Scotland.
4. Ensor, R C K, *England 1870-1914*, 1968, 77-86, The Clarendon Press, Oxford.
5. Johnstone, J C. 'Physical Training in the Army and Its Influence on British Schools', pp. 95-102 in McNair, David and Parry, Nicholas, eds, *Readings in the History of Physical Education*, 98, Autflage/First Edition Ahrensburg, 1981.
6. Ibid.

Other Books:
Cole, Lieutenant-Colonel Howard N. *The Story of Aldershot, A History and guide to Town and Camp*, 1-446, 1951, Gale and Polden Limited, Aldershot, England.
Oldfield, Lieutenant-Colonel E A L. *History of the Army Physical Training Corps*, 1-169, 1955, Gale and Polden Ltd., Aldershot.
Anderson, M S. *The Ascendancy of Europe 1815-1914*, 1-448, 2003, Third Edition, Pearson Education Limited, Harlow, Essex, England.

The general information in this appendix has been drawn from the obituaries in:
The Times, 13 March 1918, page 9 column 3.
The Army and Navy Gazette, 13 April 1918, page 239.

Other Newspapers:
Aldershot Military Gazette, 16 January 1864.
Hull Daily Mail, 21 July 1897.
Portsmouth Evening News, 15 March 1883.
Kent and Sussex Courier, 22 March 1918.
The Caledonian Mercury, 25 December 1863; 11 January 1864; 12 June 1865.
The Inverness Courier, 31 December 1863.
The Morning Post, 10 June 1871; 7 August 1875.
The Sheffield Telegraph, 24 June 1910.

Other Sources:
Register of Births, Marriages and Deaths: 1851; 1881; 1884; 1886.
England and Wales Census Returns: 1861; 1871; 1881; 1891; 1901.

APPENDIX VIII
PROGRAMME OF THE DISPLAY OF PHYSICAL TRAINING ROYAL ALBERT HALL SATURDAY 7TH JUNE 1902

LADS' DRILL ASSOCIATION.

Patron—H.R.H. THE PRINCE OF WALES.
President—THE EARL OF MEATH, P.C.

OBJECT—
(i.) Systematic Physical Training in Schools for Boys and Girls.
(ii.) The formation of Cadet Battalions and Corps throughout the Country.

AT THE ROYAL ALBERT HALL, ON Saturday, 7th June, 1902.

PROGRAMME OF THE
Display of Physical Training,

TO BE MADE IN THE PRESENCE OF THEIR ROYAL HIGHNESSES

The Prince and Princess of Wales,

In accordance with the MODEL COURSE of Physical Training prescribed by the Board of Education for Public Elementary Schools.

Chair to be taken at 2.30 by the Rt. Hon. THE EARL OF MEATH, P.C.

Price—ONE PENNY.

PROGRAMME

Extract from the MODEL COURSE issued by the Board of Education, England. (p. 23.)

The object of this training is not display, but the setting up of the scholar, and the development of his (or her) muscles and activity.

The teacher must never lose sight of the fact that his aim is the development and consequent strengthening, of the *whole* of the body, and not of one particular part. Everything depends upon the teacher, and if he is capable, it is certain that good results will ensue.

Too much importance cannot be placed on the position laid down for each exercise being rigidly adhered to. This especially holds good in "free gymnastics," where, unless the correct position is maintained, the exercise is useless, requiring no muscular exertion whatever; for instance, in bending and stretching the arms with the hands on the ground, if the body or legs are relaxed and allowed to bend, very little muscular exertion is thrown on the arms, shoulders, and the chest, and the value of the exercise is lost.

Previous to the commencement of the Programme a Display of Musical Drill will be given by the Portsmouth Garrison School.   Master—MR. DIMMOCK.

2-30.   Chair will be taken by the **RIGHT HON. THE EARL OF MEATH, P.C.**

2-40.   Portsmouth Stamshaw Board School, 64 Girls.—Calisthenic Exercises.   (Not model course.)
Instructress of Class—MISS A. RATCLIFFE.

2-50.   Heston, St. Paul's Board School, 48 Girls.—Marching Exercises and Free Gymnastics.
(Model course.)   Instructor of Class—MR. WOODS.

3-0.   Aldershot Regimental School, 48 Boys.—Marching Exercises and Free Gymnastics.
(Model course.)   Instructor of Class—MR. THOMAS.

3-10.   Haslemere National School, 48 Boys & Girls, Mixed.—Marching Exercises and Bar Bells.
(Model course.)   Instructor of Class—MR. G. H. TYLER.

3-20.   Croydon Parish Church National Schools, 48 Boys.—Marching Exercises and Dumb Bells.
(Model course.)   Instructor of Class—MR. A. BINGHAM.

PROGRAMME

3-30. Dorking British School, 48 Boys & Girls, Mixed.—Marching Exercises & Free Gymnastics. (Model course.) Instructor of Class—MR. S. COUSIN.

3-40. Colchester North Street Board School, 48 Girls and Boys, Mixed.—Marching Exercises and Free Gymnastics. (Model course.) Instructor of Class—MR. F. A. BATE.

3-50. Aldershot Regimental School, 48 Girls.—Marching Exercises and Dumb Bell Exercise. (Model course.) Instructress of Class—MRS. COGHLAN.

4-0. Portsmouth Flying Bull Lane Board School, 52 Boys.—Dumb Bell Exercises. (Model course.) Instructor of Class—MR. H. A. SMITH.

4-10. Witley King Edward's School, 60 Boys—Marching Exercises and Physical Drill with Arms. (Model course.) Instructor of Class—SERGEANT A. H. DANCE.

4-20. Woking and Guildford, 48 Lady Teachers.—Marching Exercises and Dumb Bell Exercises. (Model course.) Instructor of Class—STAFF SERGEANT W. BROWN.

4-30. Duke of York's Royal Military School, 60 Boys.—Marching Exercises and Free Gymnastics. (Model course.) Instructor of Class—COLOUR-SERGEANT LEE.

4-40. Presentation of Medals by

Their Royal Highnesses The Prince & Princess of Wales.

GOD BLESS THE PRINCE OF WALES.

GOD SAVE THE KING

LADS' DRILL ASSOCIATION.

OBJECT II.—The Formation of Cadet Battalions and Corps throughout the Country.

Africa.
MARITZBURG COLLEGE CADET.

By kind permission of the Proprietors of the Sketch.

Field-Marshal Lord Roberts addressing the Cadets at Pietermaritzburg said:
"I hope the old Country will follow the example of one of her children and *insist* upon all boys joining Cadet Corps."

Scotland.

Extract from a circular letter, dated February 3rd, 1900, forwarded by the Scottish Educational Department to School Boards and Managers of Schools in Scotland.

SIR,—I am directed by Lord Balfour of Burleigh, to bring under the attention of School Boards and Managers of schools a subject which is one of great public importance, and which in his Lordship's opinion concerns not less the interests of the pupils of State-aided schools than the welfare and security of the Empire. It is that of physical exercise, and particularly of those forms of military drill which most effectively develop the physical capacities of the pupils and train them in the habit of the combined and dexterous employment of those capacities.

Lord Balfour is convinced that such exercises, apart from any other consideration, would be a most important aid in attaining some substantial objects at which all education must aim. Not only do they tend to improve manual dexterity, and to render more alert the facilities of observation, but they are also pre-eminently useful in developing those habits of comradeship, of responsibility, and of individual resource, which are of supreme importance, not only to the nation as a whole, but to the individual pupil.

In his speech at the Guildhall, on the 5th December, 1901, H.R.H. The Prince of Wales, made use of the following noticeable words:

"I am anxious to refer to an admirable movement which has taken strong root in both Australia and New Zealand—that is the establishment of Cadet Corps. On several occasions I had the gratification of seeing march past several thousand cadets armed and equipped, and who, at the expense of their respective Governments, are able to go through a military course, in some cases with an ample grant of practice ammunition. I will not presume in these days of army reform, to do more than call the attention of my friend, the Secretary for War, to this interesting fact."

Australia.
A VICTORIAN CADET.

Dr. Morrison, Principal of the Presbyterian College, Melbourne, in an address presented to H.R.H. the Prince of Wales, said:—"We have striven to send forth from our Schools good and true men, loyal and patriotic citizens, who will not only do their work well in every social, civil and religious capacity, but will fight if need be for their King and Country, as so many of our old boys recently have fought."

Murray & Co., Printers, 180, Brompton Road, S.W.

APPENDIX IX
A SHORT INTRODUCTION TO THE EDUCATION
(PROVISION OF MEALS) ACT, 1906

The Education (Provision of Meals), 1906, marked a significant change in the welfare provision for elementary schoolchildren attending Public Elementary Schools first established by the 1870 Act. The 1906 Act was permissive in character, i.e. it established powers but no duties on Leas, themselves established by the 1902 Act. They could raise a halfpenny (½d.) rate provided they received approval from the Board of Education to do so. In its permissive character, it followed the principle of the first Public Health Act, 1848, which was also permissive in all essentials.

A later Education (Provision of Meals) Act, 1914, abolished the necessity for Leas to apply to the Board to implement a regime of school meals provision in their local area. Nevertheless, Leas could opt in or out year by year and by the time of the Education Act, 1921, and also by 1939, there were Leas that had never implemented the 1906 Act at all.

In essence, however, the 1906 Act was an education act since its primary purpose was to ensure that elementary schoolchildren were no longer to be deprived of profiting from the education provided through the lack of insufficiency of food.[1] It also opened the door for the 1907 Act, which, under Sections 13(1)(b) and 13(2) established the School Medical Service from 1 January 1908 under the auspices of Sir George Newman who, as CMO subsequently incorporated the 1906 Act as a characteristic constituent of a Public Health approach to the administration of the SMS, to which his appointment had been directed.

The fact was that the 1906 Act and the establishment of the SMS by the 1907 Act, were, in effect, like the 1902 Act and the various elementary Acts passed subsequent to the 1870 Act, designed to fill the gaps of the educational and welfare deficiencies originally neglected in 1870. Two welfare deficiencies had been legally provided for under the 1893 and 1899 Acts. Yet, throughout the period 1870-1906 there were no other legal or political attempts to establish any form of health care for elementary schoolchildren. Indeed, the 1902 Act was an act of structural, educational administrative reform, which, crucially enabled Newman to develop health and welfare services for elementary schoolchildren within the context of the Leas established by the act.

Nevertheless, social conditions prior to the 1906 Act had prompted many charitable school meal initiatives of an individual and local nature, which, in their turn, were also followed by initiatives from individual schools and School Boards, the precursors of leas, leading to the establishment of voluntary agencies both inside and outside of the PES in the provision of meals for children. This ad hoc approach, especially in the larger towns and cities, and campaigns by institutions like the National Union of Teachers (NUT) eventually led to political debate in parliament and elsewhere to the eventual passing of the 1906 Act.

Notes
1. Board of Education, *Circular 552*, 1 January 1907, 1.

APPENDIX X
MEMORANDUM ON PHYSICAL TRAINING PRACTICAL SUGGESTIONS PRINCIPALLY FOR RURAL SCHOOLS[1]

1. Instruction

    (a)   As a general rule physical training should be carried on by the teachers forming the ordinary school staff rather than by outside instructors.......They must, however, first learn to instruct. For this purpose, groups of Schools can combine to secure the services of a qualified instructor, who should, if possible have been trained in the Army Gymnastic course.......The War Office have recently issued instructions to all General Officers Commanding Districts, providing for the employment, by voluntary arrangement, of qualified Non-Commissioned Officers as instructors of teachers' classes..... A copy of the War Office letter, with a list of Commanding Officers, is subjoined.

In addition to the assistance thus given by the War Office, it has been decided by a private society – the Lads' Drill Association – to use a certificate of competency to teachers who satisfy their tests as instructors in the Model Course.........

The following is the War Office letter to General Officers Commanding Districts referred to above [para 1 (a)] :-

                      War Office, London S.W.
                      2nd Jul, 1902.

Sir,

I am directed by the Commander-in-Chief to inform you that a Model Course of Physical Training has, after consultation with this Office, been proposed for use at Schools under the jurisdiction of the Board of Education.

2. It is highly desirable that these schools should be trained to impart instruction in the proposed Course of Physical Training.

3. Lord Roberts has approved of facilities being offered to the Educational Authorities or School Managers who desire to employ competent Non-commissioned Officers is voluntary, *and that it in no way interferes with their military duties.*

4. Subject to the above conditions, Classes of Instruction for Teachers at Schools, who may apply to attend, may be formed either at any of the established or modified gymnasia in your district, or at any centre which may be selected by

arrangement between yourself and Educational Authorities or Teachers. Each class should consist of about 20 or 30 members, and be held in the evenings, preferably Saturday evening, or a Saturday morning, which would usually be most convenient to Teachers.

5. No expense of Army Funds will be incurred, but each Instructor employed will make his own agreement in regard to remuneration and repayment of expenses. In order that a uniform scale may, as far as possible, be adopted, 3d per head per lesson of one hour, with a fixed minimum for each lesson, is suggested.

6. I am to request you to make the necessary arrangements for the formation of the above classes. It has been suggested by the Board of Education that Managers of Schools should communicate on the subject direct with you, or with the Officers Commanding Regimental Depots.

7. If necessary, you will correspond direct with the Secretary, Board of Education, Whitehall, London, S.W.,

                I am Sir,
                Your Obedient Servant,

                J.K. Kenny
                Adjutant-General to the Forces.

The General Officer Commanding.

Note
1. *School Board Chronicle*, Volume LXVIII, 30 August 1902, 214-215.

APPENDIX XI
A DIARY OF SIR THOMAS LAUDER BRUNTON'S PROPOSED LEAGUE FOR PE AND IMPROVEMENT

Sir Thomas Lauder Brunton was born on 14 March 1844 and died 16 September 1916. (His biographical details may be found on http://thepeerage.com/p18641.htm). His early skirmishes into his beliefs concerning PE was basically that of military training for boys,[1] which were published in a series of articles.[2]

One of these skirmishes was in a letter *The Times*[3] in which he responded to the poem *The Islanders* published in *The Times*[4].

In his letter, he advocated that childish games, such as 'I Spy', 'French and English' and 'Prisoners' Base' – old war games of scouting, capture and recapture, be adapted to the necessities of modern warfare:

> "let all children be taught at school partly in play and partly as work how to handle a gun, how to shoot and how to manoeuvre"[5]

In January 1903, *The Lancet* published a leader,[6] which acknowledged the article by General Sir Frederick Maurice entitled *National Health: A Soldier's Study*.[7] The crux of Maurice's argument was that under the voluntary system of recruitment for the army, (in contrast to Continental conscription), for every five men offering themselves, only two were made into effective soldiers.[8] This failure rate was due: (a) to flat feet making marching impossible; (b) bad teeth, which were the prime reason for recruits being unable to digest their food; (c) early marriages, which were unable to feed and sustain children adequately.[9] Maurice concluded that the mental, moral and physical conditions endured by women and children were the conspicuous deficiencies in regard "to the future of our land".[10]

In its response, a leader in *The Lancet*[11] suggested that the national health had been unfairly impeached[12] by Maurice. Moreover, the national health was, in fact, improving,[13] while indicating that the recruits noted by Maurice were drawn from that part of the population where the general improvements in health, had not, so far, had any marked effect. Furthermore, they had no particular aptitude for any trade or profession.

On 14 February 1903, *The Lancet*[14], published a letter of support in the editorial from Sir Lauder Brunton, physician to St Bartholomew's Hospital. Nevertheless, Brunton suggested that a small commission be appointed to inquire into a limited number of points raised by Maurice concerning the national health, viz., bad teeth, flat feet and generally weak physique.[15]

Meanwhile, on 6 July 1903,[16] a debate on the 1903 Report took place in the House of Lords, in which, the Earl of Meath, the Bishop of Ripon, the Duke of Devonshire (the Lord President of the Council) and the Earl of Mansfield, who had been chairman of the Royal Commission that published the 1903 Report, spoke. The Duke of Devonshire, who replied for the government, indicated that consultations in regard to further enquiries, were to take place concerning the appointment of another Royal Commission into the matters of national physique and health.[17]

On 14 July 1903, Brunton again wrote to *The Lancet*[18], commending a report in the *Manchester Guardian*[19] by John Burns (1858-1943), who wrote:

"The father must drink less alcohol and the mother less tea, take more exercise and suckle her children."[20]

After advocating various remedies, he suggested that a national league to promote physical development – which had been in draft form for over a year, but, owing to illness, and a death, had been delayed – be then ripe for bringing to fruition.[21]

In a House of Commons question,[22] Balfour replied that an enquiry concerning a Royal Commission on PT could not be determined without further consideration. Brunton had also written to the BMJ[23] on 14 July 1903 on *A Health Conscience and A National League for Physical Education*.

Subsequently, John Black Atkins, editor of the *Manchester Guardian* reported on a dinner given by Brunton, which outlined the basis on which the proposed league was to take place.[24] The dinner was also reported in *The Lancet*.[25]

On 14 September 1903, it was reported that a committee had been appointed to make a preliminary inquiry into statements that had been made regarding the physical deterioration of certain classes of the population in the United Kingdom.[26] Among its members was Colonel Fox.

The 1904 Report reported on 20 July 1904.[27] Subsequently, *The Lancet* interpreted, in three separate articles,[28] its interpretations of the findings of the 1904 Report.

On 13 August 1904, however, Brunton again wrote to *The Lancet*, even though it had, up to that point, only published one of the three articles. The reason for his haste seems to have been one of regret at the findings, and, he again envisaged a proposed National League for Physical Education and Improvement.[29]

In the interim, the *Report of the Inter-Departmental Committee on the Model Course of Physical Exercises* had reported on 10 March 1904.[30]

From that Report sprang *Circular 515* dd 22 August 1904, in which the 1904 Syllabus was advocated,[31] a report of which also figured in *The Times*.[32]

In November 1904, The Lancet reported that:

"on the 16 November 1904 an initial conference was to be held in the London Education Offices to consider the possibility of establishing for England, a national or central school for Physical Education on the lines of the Royal Central Institute for Sweden.[33]

Brunton was among those that attended that meeting. The envisaged scheme was described by Miss Theodora Johnson, Principal of the Swedish Institute, Clifton.[34] Also there was Lord Londonderry, President of the Board of Education, but not in an official capacity.[35] Nevertheless, there were implications for PT to merge with military training.[36]

Brunton, however, was clearly discontented at developments and addressed a meeting of headteachers,[37] on the proposed National League in which the sub-headings were: migration from the country to the towns; how to maintain people in the country; effects of alcohol; personal hygiene; PT; military training; proper feeding; help of teachers; cooperation of workers and the proposed League. Brunton delivered a further speech on the subject.[38]

The League was eventually inaugurated on Wednesday 28 June 1905 at the Mansion House at which the Lord Mayor presided.[39] Donations totalled £815. 1s. 0d. Among those who contributed were General Sir Frederick Maurice (KCB) (£10. 10s. 0d.); the Earl of Meath (£5. 5s. 0d.); Colonel Fox (£5.5s. 0d.); Sir Henry Craik (KCB) (£2. 2s. 0d.); The Reverend E. Warre DD (£2. 2s. 0d.); Miss Theodora Johnson (£1. 1s. 0d.) and F H Grenfell (£1. 1s. 0d.).

The Provisional Executive Council consisted of forty-four members. The Chairman was the Bishop of Ripon; Alfred Hoare, Honorary Treasurer; J E Walker Hon Solicitor; Beverley Halley, Secretary.

Other members were: Sir James Crichton-Browne, MD LL.D, FRS; Sir Lauder Brunton, MD, D. Sc., LL.D, FRS; The Bishop of Bristol; The Bishop of Hereford; Major-General Sir Frederick Maurice, KCB; The Lord Mayor of London; Sir Henry Craik, KCB; Right Honourable Sir John E. Gorst, PC, MP; T J Macnamara, LL.D, MP; Reverend Edmond Warre, CB, DD; John Black Atkins; E H Pooley, late secretary to the Inter-Departmental Committee on Physical Deterioration; C B Fry, BA; Eustace Miles, MA; Pelham Warner.

The Objects of the League[38]

1. To stimulate public interest in the Physical Condition of the People throughout the United Kingdom.
2. To establish close Association and Centralisation of all Societies and individuals trying to combat such influences as tend to produce National Physical Deterioration.
3. To aid existing Organisations.
4. To start Organisations for Physical Health and well-being wherever none exists.

Notes

1. Penn, Alan, *Targeting Schools, Drill, Militarism and Imperialism*, 81-3, Woburn Press, London, 1999.
2. Brunton, Lauder. *Collected Papers on Physical and Military Training*, Published from 10 Stratford Place, 1887-1915, 1915.
3. *The Times*, 7 January 1902, 10.
4. Ibid., 4 January 1902, 9.
5. Ibid.
6. *The Lancet*, 31 January 1903, 315-7.
7. Maurice, Frederick. 'National Health: A Soldier's Study', in *The Contemporary Review*, Volume LXXXIII, 41-56, January-June, 1903.
8. Ibid., 42.
9. Ibid., 41-7.
10. Ibid., 50.
11. *The Lancet*, op. cit., 31 January, 1903.
12. Ibid., 316.
13. Ibid.
14. *The Lancet*, 14 February 1903, 471.
15. Ibid.
16. *Hansard*, House of Lords, 6 July 1903, columns 1324-54.
17. *The Lancet*, 11 July 1903, 133.
18. Ibid., 18 July 1903, 185.

19. *The Manchester Guardian*, 27 April 1903.
20. *The Lancet*, op. cit., 18 July 1903, 185.
21. Ibid.
22. *Hansard*, Volume 125, 4th. Series, Commons Questions, 15 July 1903, column 694.
23. *British Medical Journal*, 18 July 1903.
24. *The Manchester Guardian*, 23 July 1903, 12.
25. *The Lancet*, 25 July 1903, 250.
26. *BMJ*, 14 September 1903, 607.
27. HMSO, Command 2175, *Report of the Inter-Departmental Committee on Physical Deterioration*, 1-93.
28. *The Lancet*, (A) 6 August 1904, 391-392. (B) 20 August 1904, 557-8. (C) 10 September 1904, 785-7.
29. Ibid., 13 August 1904, 487.
30. HMSO, Command 2032, 411, *Report of the Inter-Departmental Committee on the Model Course of Physical Exercises*, 1-9.
31. Board of Education, *Circular 515*, 22 August 1904.
32. *The Times*, 23 August 1904, 8.
33. *The Lancet*, 12 November 1904, 1367.
34. Ibid.
35. *The Times*, 17 November 1904, 7.
36. Ibid.
37. Brunton, Lauder. 'Address on a National League to the Federation of Head Teachers at Cambridge', 5 January 1905 in *Collected Papers*, op. cit., 1915.
38. 'Notes on the Objects of the League and an Account of The Inauguration of the League at the Mansion House', 28 June 1905, in *Collected Papers*, op. cit., 1915.

APPENDIX XII
RESPONSES TO THE APPOINTMENT OF MAJOR NORMAN

On 20 October 1906, a letter appeared in *The Schoolmaster* (p. 705) referring to the appointment of Major Norman. A fortnight later a further letter appeared (3 November 1906 p. 792; *The Schoolmaster*) in support of the former. Both were published under the pseudonyms of Senex and Sinjun, respectively. Both were critical of aspects of the appointment.

According to the former contributor, a circular issued by the SEC concerning the appointment of Major Norman noted that the Superintendent was to have the services of an assistant Army Sergeant. The duties of the Superintendent included the inspection of physical training in all the elementary schools under the control of the SEC. He was also to draw up reports regarding the efficiency of the instruction and the capabilities of the teachers *in their latest role* (author's italics) of Instructors of Physical Training. The sergeant assistant was also empowered to visit schools and report to the Superintendent. Then, says Senex, came the following remarkable specimen of bureaucratic wisdom:

"As the discipline and tone shown at the time of physical instruction must bear an important relation to that of the school as a whole, or any particular class in the school, it follows that the reports of the superintendent will deal incidentally with this important matter, and will be taken into account by my committee when considering the general efficiency of instruction and the qualification of the teachers throughout their area."

The gentlemen responsible for this communication, said Senex, where they would make drill and and discipline interchangeable terms, blundered. Such a blunder would not have been committed by the rawest recruit of the teaching profession.

In an even more critical passage Senex made an accusation which would receive condemnation today:

"As your readers are well aware, perfect drill may be obtained under a degrading system of terrorism, and such drill might gain the highest commendation from an Army inspector. But the tone of such a school would be deplorable."

The best judges of tone and discipline, had in the past, been His Majesty's Inspector but apparently this had all been changed. The peaceful pedagogues of the past had now to face a metamorphosis into military martinets, or their chances of promotion, microscopic though they were, would grow smaller by degrees and beautifully less!

Many Surrey teachers were presently attending the Authority's scheme of physical training expending time and money and travelling long distances to attend classes of instruction in the subject. Nevertheless, those same teachers felt that drill should occupy a subordinate place in the curriculum and should not dominate the whole. The drill inspectors should stick to reporting on the drill. The sooner the SEC withdrew the objectionable clauses in the circular, the better, since, as presently construed, it was an insult to teachers and HMIs.

Sinjun described, in the opening of his letter, the letter from Senex as "admirable". Nevertheless, apart from the soldier in the school, an evil which was not to be tolerated, the whole question of physical exercises required consideration. Quoting a paragraph in the *Grand Magazine* by Dr Alexander Bryce, Sinjun raised the question of army recruitment:

> "In Sweden - the foremost gymnastic country in the world - one-third of the population dies before the age of twenty-one, and, of the males who are left one-quarter are rejected for military service."

Sinjun, then goes on to suggest that the introduction of the syllabus being forced on pupils, teachers and schools administered by the SEC was ill-considered in so far as the SEC regarded themselves as 'educationalists' and failed to ask the following questions.

1. How many schools under the authority possessed central halls? Without such halls it was impossible to drill regularly and effectively. Wet days, excessively hot days and bitterly cold days rendered playgrounds unsuitable for physical exercises.

2. Was the clothing of the children generally suited to the exercise? This question, said Sinjun, should have been considered in conjunction with the illustrated official syllabus.

3. Did all children derive benefit from the exercises and were the exercises injurious to children? Some children in scattered communities walked many miles to and from school; others, of nervous temperament, are positively injured by the strain of fixed movements at word of command. Sinjun relates that, at his/her school, a boy fainted after fifteen minutes physical exercise in a hot playground, and others showed signs of distress.

4. Should infants be subjected to formal exercises at the word of command? It had been said, Sinjun noted, that a male expert had expressed the view that two hours a week be devoted to the subject in infant schools. What did infant teachers say?

5. How many teachers have suffered from colds and temporary loss of voice through leaving warm rooms to stand for half-an-hour in an unpaved playground on cold and damp days?

These were not the only questions to ask and no doubt there were other questions, Sinjun observed, which others might have, but, these and others should have been thought of prior to the imposition of physical exercises on all schools alike whether or not the buildings were ancient or modern; whether or not the district was urban or rural; whether or not the children from varying ages, temperaments and strength (the well-fed and the ill-fed, the well clothed and the badly clothed) be fitted or unfitted to take part in the exercises common to the class in which they were placed for other subjects of instruction.

It is to be noted that the SCC and the SEC on receipt of *Circular 515* dd 22 August 1904 appointed both a Superintendent of Physical Training and an Educational Medical Officer in the shape of Dr Thomas Henry Jones, both of whom were appointed in July 1905.[1]

Notes

1. Pegg J R, 'In Sickness and In Health: The Origins and Systematic Development of Children's Medical Inspection and Treatment in the County of Surrey's Public Elementary Schools 1905-1921, Pioneered by Dr Thomas Henry Jones, A Documentary History', Studies in the History of Surrey Schools Volume 1, Angela Blaydon Publishing Ltd, 2017.

APPENDIX XIII
ATTENDANCES AT PT COURSES & CERTIFICATES AWARDED AND INSPECTIONS MADE BY COLONEL FOX

Note: The individual numbers quoted in the reports do not always tally with total numbers quoted either in attendance or certificates awarded.

Place	No. of Classes	Dates Commenced	Dates Completed	No. of Lessons	Attendances Men	Attendances Women	Attendances Total	Certificates Women	Certificates Men	Certificates Total	Col Fox Inspected*
Sutton	(2)	11-11-05	? March 06				}369	96	20	116	12-03-06
Guildford	(2)	12-11-05	? March 06				}	82	27	109	13-03-06
Wimbledon	(2)	25-09-05	? May 06		9		106	61	9	70	10-05-06*
Haslemere				25		7	7	5		5	---
Kingston	(2)	March 06	Dec. 06	30					}	#	02-10-06*
Woking	(2)	March 06	Dec. 06	30					}		21-11-06*
Farnham	(2)	March 06	Dec. 06	25				265	90}	355	30-11-06*
Dorking		11-04-06	Dec. 06	30					}		12-11-06*
										655**	
Richmond			Dec. 07	25			156				
Caterham			Dec. 07	25			105				
Lingfield			Dec. 07	20			35				
								702	183	885***	
Mortlake		01-08?								19	
Redhill		13-01-08								77	
					360	1244	1604^	702	183	953****	
Horley								22	4	26	
								724	187	979*****	
Mitcham		19-06-08	19-01-09	23	99	122		45	12	57	22-12-08*
Egham		24-06-08	03-02-09	24	52	76		27	13	40	16-12-08*
							1876<<<	>>>1087			
Epsom	(2)	22-03-09	08-11-09	40	120	160		54	32	86+	11-10-09*
Guildford	(2)	23-03-09	02-11-09	54	174	228		80	29	109+	12-10-09*
Camberley		25-03-09	11-11-09	20	60	80		38	10	48+	14-10-09*
Kingston (practical & written course)	(7)	18-11-09	23-06-10	85	275	360		122	49	171+	23-06-10*

* = authorised endorsement by Colonel Fox.
\# This date was quoted by Colonel Fox in the 18th Report of the SEC. Major Norman, however, had reported in Appendix E.2 dd. 14th September 1906 that the Kingston class had already been inspected.
** Major Norman reported in Appendix E.3 dd. 3-1-07 in the 18th Report of the SEC that the total number of certificates was 643.

***	Appendix M.1 Report of the Supt. of PT dd. 2 January 1908 in 22nd Report of the SEC notes 16 teachers not included in the figures as they were attending a class for the second time.
****	The number of certificates awarded so far was quoted in Appendix M.1 Report of the Assistant Instructor of PT dd. 30 September 1908 in 25th Report of the SEC.
*****	The number of certificates quoted as awarded in Appendix M.1 Report of the Assistant Instructor of PT dd. 24th November 1908 in the 26th Report of the SEC
<<<	The number of total attendances quoted in Appendix M.1 30th September 1908 in 25th Report of the SEC.
>>>	The number of certificates awarded in Appendix M.1 Report of the Superintendent of PT dd. 31 January 1909 in the 27th Report of the SEC
^	Appendix M.3 n.d. Report of the Superintendent of PT in the 23rd Report of the SEC
+	Epsom 28 teachers already held certificates (1 man 27 women)
+	Guildford 28 teachers already held certificates (6 men 22 women)
+	Camberley – 4 women previously held certificates
+	Kingston 91 teachers previously held certificates (14 men 77women) 60 teachers (12 men 48 women) had their old certificates endorsed

The Superintendent also held a series of one-off classes in order to help teachers adjust to the 1909 Syllabus:

Redhill	135	Barnes	70	Mitcham	120	Dorking	76
Cranleigh	25	Haslemere	21	Lingfield	25	Godalming	60
Farnham	80	Guildford	144	Woking	124	Camberley	53
Sutton	129	Purley	77	Epsom	76	Chertsey	65
Egham	55	Oxted	33	Horley	35		

A total of 1403 teachers attended; 700 of whom held County certificates.

All the classes were held in the evening except Lingfield, Purley and Oxted which took place on Saturday mornings.

The duration of each class was 2½ hours except Dorking, Haslemere, Godalming, Camberley and Oxted, which were 2¼ hours and Horley, which was 2 hours.

APPENDIX XIV
A BIOGRAPHY OF CAPTAIN F H GRENFELL AND HIS VIEWS ON SWEDISH GYMNASTICS

Francis Henry Grenfell DSO (1875-1946) was born in January 1875 at Alverstoke, Hampshire. He died on 29 April 1946 at Miller General Hospital, Greenwich, London. He never married.

In the 1881 census, aged six, he was resident at 2 Oak Villa, Bury Road, Alverstoke. Ten years later, his address in the census was stated as Shanklin, Isle of Wight and was described as a midshipman from 15 May 1891 in the Royal Navy (RN).

In this regard, he was following in the family tradition of service in the RN. His father, Hubert Henry Grenfell, Captain, RN, was born in Rugby, Warwickshire on 12 June 1845. At his death on 13 September 1906, he resided at 5 Anglesey Crescent, Crescent Road, Alverstoke, Hampshire. Grenfell's mother, Eleanor Kate Cunningham was born on 10 August 1852 in Alverstoke, almost certainly at Bury House. She outlived her husband by a further twenty-six years.

In early September 1882, H H Grenfell was captain of the British warship *HMS Phoenix*, which had a complement of about 140-150 men.[1] The ship was on route from Quebec to Halifax when she encountered heavy seas as she approached East Point on Prince Edward Island. She ran aground on the reef extending from East Point.[2]

On running aground, the ship was lost but there was no loss of life. The salvage rights to the wreck were sold for £3,000.[3]

Prior to 1882 there had been many requests from naval and governmental sources for a lighthouse to be built at East Point.[4] Eventually one was built in 1866/67[5] but several modifications had subsequently to be made to the lighting of the lighthouse[6].

Nevertheless, the court of enquiry ruled that the stranding of the *Phoenix* was due to negligent navigation, citing, as a reason for condemnation, a disregard for the taking of proper precautions regarding the correct determination of the distance of the ship from the light of the lighthouse. Commander Grenfell was given a severe reprimand and dismissed ship.[7]

Even so, there was clearly some doubt about the validity of the judgment in view of the modifications to the lighting of the lighthouse, its siting,[8] prior to 1882, and to later modifications of the alarm systems[9] and the siting.

Although Hubert Henry was not granted another command after the loss of the *Phoenix*, he was later promoted to captain. From the time of the loss of the *Phoenix*, it is clear that he sought to recover his career. Following the loss of the Phoenix and other ships, in particular the loss of the *SS Quebec* in 1879, the lighthouse was moved in 1885 to the place where it appeared on the chart. (*see* the East Point Lighthouse website). From 1886 to 1903 evidence suggests that twenty patents were issued in his name, almost all to do with naval matters and gunnery.[10] In 1892 he was in partnership with James Accles, who is better known as the partner of Pollock, founders of a well-known company. His main work during that time was on naval ordnance. His address on the patents is given as: 1886-1888 Newcastle upon Tyne, 1891-1901 various addresses in London and from 1901 to 1903 Alverstoke.

~~~~~~~

The Naval Lists indicate that Francis Henry Grenfell was promoted to Lieutenant 14 September 1894. Subsequently, an account of Grenfell's early career in the RN's Gymnastic Department set up in 1902 at Portsmouth, indicate that his association and attachment to the Swedish System of Exercises was formed and cemented as first assistant superintendent to Commander N C Palmer.[11]

On leaving the navy, Grenfell undertook the introduction of Swedish Drill into the Public Schools, including Eton.[12]

This work gave an impetus to his appointment as HMI of PT to the Board in 1909. Advantageous to his appointment was Newman's affection for the Swedish System.[13]

In 1914, Grenfell rejoined the navy and was promoted Commander on 8 December 1914. For the first year of the war he served a year as Second in Command of the armed merchant cruiser *Cedric* in the 10th Cruiser Squadron made up of Armed Merchant Ships. He volunteered for Q ships and was given command of *HMS Penshurst*. He proved very successful in several naval actions. He accounted for two enemy submarines, the UB-19 and UB-37.[14] The photograph of the piece of German Shrapnel is from UB 37[15] with an account of the incident in the following photograph (*see* Colour Plates XIV and XV).[16]

For those services he was awarded the DSO, 1 January 1917, to which a bar was added on 23 March 1917. He also received the French Croix de Guerre. On 8 March 1917, he was promoted to captain.

On returning to the Board after the First World War, he continued as the Chief Inspector of PT. Retiring at the age of sixty, Grenfell developed his talents in mountaineering and music. He acquired a significant art collection of modern etchings. Subsequently, he developed an interest in sculpting, and, after eighteen months of training had some of his work accepted for the Royal Academy.[17]

~~~~~~~

Lieutenant-Commander Grenfell was appointed by George Newman to the inspectorate of the School Medical Service in 1908 and was appointed His Majesty's Inspector of Physical Training in 1909.[18]

Grenfell's article[19] on Swedish Drill reflects a paean of praise for Ling and the Swedish System of Exercises. It was, he noted, the result of a century of effort. Swedish Gymnastics was a logical whole and to discard any of its main features would mean that what was left would not be worth very much.

He based his comments on the instruction and practice at the Royal Gymnastic Central Institute and in the schools of Stockholm. The references to the history and growth of the system were founded upon memoranda of conversions with Professor Tongren and other gymnasts.

The Swedish physical training claimed a place as a serious factor in the general education of the child. In order to justify this claim it had to be shown that the Swedish system was a rational and complete physical training ensuring a normal development of all organs and their functions culminating in physical perfection.

It can be observed that the next part of his essay was a rationale of justification for this notion of the achievement of physical perfection by Swedish Gymnastics, and, was, in this sense, a vindication for its introduction into the elementary schools as a means of eliminating all those anatomical and physiological problems that had beset army recruitment for some considerable time and exposed by the Boer War.

Thus:

"Physical Training, from this point of view, is largely a corrective for the damage resulting from civilised conditions, and must be competent to deal with subnormal subjects if economically efficient."

Not only that, but Swedish Gymnastics, rightly conceived, also had claims to character-formation:

"The power of self-control, both in expression and repose, may be strengthened; determination, courage and perseverance can be cultivated, and so can quickness of decision and correctness of judgment; in fact, proper physical training goes a long way to form the good citizen."

If this was reminiscent of Edwin Chadwick's notions of Drill (Appendix II), nevertheless, Grenfell insisted that the Swedish concept of physical training could only be rational when grounded upon the facts of the construction and life-processes of the body, and upon the nature of its physical and mental development. It was, therefore, necessary to take account of the fact of these developments in the growing child and, adjusted in the physical training of the children, according to the changes taking place in the mental and physical capacities of each child at different stages of growth.

In one sense, one can see why the issue of sport does not appear as a more substantial approach in the various *Syllabi of Physical Training* issued by the Board of Education. A child's physical and mental well-being was dependent upon the concept of the *whole-man* since the various sporting rules did not change with these growing capacities. Indeed, the *Syllabus of Physical Training for Schools*, 1933, issued by the Board of Education embracing 352 pages devotes Chapter IV to The Organisation and Coaching of Games, a total of twenty-four pages and Chapter IX, Description of Games and Practices, a total of sixty-seven pages. "Sport" only occurs in reference to Sports Days.

Nevertheless, Grenfell acknowledges that games have a part to play within the concept of Swedish Gymnastics. The games, he postulated, were divided into either gymnastic or pedagogical, and true and free games. The former were more gymnastic in character, and, as a result, were controlled, more or less, by the teacher. Nevertheless all games had an educational purpose. Thus the games had various aims such as 'sharpening the attention' or for alertness at the right moment or for speed in running and starting, or for climbing and balancing and for endurance, precision of aim or nimbleness. In order to reach these various stages of competence the games themselves were divided into ring games, song games, running games, as in catching and racing. Then there were ball-games including football, hockey, etc., and throwing games, such as will-spear, quoits and ball-catching. Contest games were those such as tug-of-war, wrestling and so on.

For the youngest children imagination was required as well as giving them plenty of scope for imitation. Boys' games for older children ought to be directed to competition and contest including running and song games, climbing and obstacle races undertaken in the gymnasium and would be based on individual and team permutations. Girls' games were much more peaceful in character, yet, lively in application and included ring and chain games, skipping, dancing action and song games. Dancing, in particular, was appreciated by the girls but they were prepared with care and based on a progression of gymnastic exercises leading to dancing that produced "beautiful effects".

Similarly, the use of gymnastic training and gymnastic exercises was a preparation for swimming, diving, wrestling and pole jumping before their actual application for gymnastics. Accordingly, preparatory dry-land swimming exercises enabled the children to take to the water like ducks and in no time at all were able "to pass the test of 150 metres with the greatest of ease".

In his panegyric, Grenfell accords the foundation of the scientific system of gymnastics to Ling, who established its two main divisions: pedagogical and medical, while McIntosh suggests (p. 98) that it was his son who developed the educational aspect of his system. The former was assigned its true purpose of promoting the health of mind and body, which had also been a strong element in GutsMuths concept of physical education. Nevertheless, Ling's achievement was the formulation of the characteristic types of exercises essential to the harmonious training of the body. Nevertheless, for young children, the movement of the body was the necessary component in all its different parts was achieved through different forms of games, or game-forms of the regular exercises, such as running, climbing and jumping.

As the children grew, a more directive form of exercise was required; nevertheless, these might be interspersed with games. These might include climbing on ropes and ladders, easy forms of jumping and preparatory forms of swimming exercises.

Later in their puberty, with the rapid increase of weight and height a more disciplined and stricter form of exercise was required with a definite command structure. As the body-form increased in strength the movements generated in these exercises could be seen in the context of external forms of movement, such as fencing, wrestling, racing, pole-jumping and dancing. Vaulting, in particular, could provide an exciting continuum of the progressive nature of Swedish Gymnastics.

In 1939 Grenfell offered his assessment[20] on various matters concerning PT in the elementary schools, which, for Grenfell, was the process of building bodies and personalities of school children by means of regulated physical exercise. That process was endemic within all schools over which the Board had control, although later in his review he criticizes the standards and progress in secondary schools.

His assessment of PT in the elementary schools, however, was encouraging and favourable. Instruction in particular had shown continuous and gratifying improvement over a long period of time and the teachers were to be congratulated for the earnestness with which they had approached the work. Economic difficulties in respect of apparatus and equipment had, to an extent, hampered progress. These were mainly in the areas of suitable rooms for formal physical exercises and of properly laid-out playing fields for games. These considerations had an impact on teachers in the manner of reduced enthusiasm and the tendency for innovation to stagnate.

> "Nevertheless, there is now a system that in its totality may well be described as British. Its effective application demands an expenditure that is reasonable in the light of benefits to the national health. Moreover, there are a number of Leas which have made an excellent contribution to the development of games, athletics and swimming. The towns and cities have an advantage over rural districts with regard to playing fields as children in the former can be transported into areas with appropriate facilities.

However, some Leas employ a form of economy inconsistent with the best practice of enhancing the physicality of the children since they do not employ organisers of expertise. To its credit, and to obviate the problems brought on by a failure to enhance a progressive PT curriculum, the Board has established grants in aid of salaries and expenses. The enabling of the prevention and correcting innumerable physical defects and of securing will power, strong and active citizens are the positive benefits of effective organization of PT.

In spite of the deficiencies exercised by some Leas, however, PT given in the elementary schools of this country constitutes a comprehensive and effective national service, such as will easily stand comparison with any standard that is attainable abroad:

'indeed it may be asked where else may be found a scheme of physical training so truly national, so universally employed, so generous in its scope, so consistently developed over a long course of years, so well adapted to the production of strong, healthy, self-controlled, self-reliant individuals, able to cooperate harmoniously with others in free association for rational ends' "

Photograph of F.H. Grenfell. Grateful thanks to Frank Grenfell, nephew of Captain Grenfell, for supplying and allowing use of this picture for publication

Lieutenant Commander Grenfell

Portrait of Francis Grenfell, aged 20, by his sister Florence. Grateful thanks to Frank Grenfell, nephew of Captain Grenfell, for supplying and allowing use of this picture for publication

Photograph of HMS Penshurst. *Grateful thanks to Frank Grenfell, nephew of Captain Grenfell, for supplying and allowing use of this picture*

Death Certificate of F.H. Grenfell. Grateful thanks to Frank Grenfell, nephew of Captain Grenfell, for supplying and allowing use of this document

Sculpture exhibited at The Royal Academy by F.H. Grenfell. Photograph of F.H. Grenfell. Grateful thanks to Frank Grenfell, nephew of Captain Grenfell, for supplying and allowing use of this picture

Notes

1. http://enwikipedia.org/wiki/HMS_Phoenix_%281879%29
2. http://www.lighthousefriends.com/light.asp?ID=945
3. http://enwikipedia op. cit.
4. http://www.lighthouse op. cit.
5. Ibid.
6. Ibid.
7. http://enwikipedia op. cit.
8. http://wwwlighthouse op. cit.
9. Ibid.
10. Private communication from Frank Grenfell 15 October 2014
11. Mcintosh, Peter C. *Physical Education in England since 1800*,156-158, Bell and Hyman, Revised & Enlarged Edition, London, 1968.
12. Ibid.
13. Ibid.
14. http://enwikipedia.org/wiki/HMSPenshurst
15. Private communication from Frank Grenfell.
16. Ibid.
17. http://www.grenfellhistory.co.uk/biographies//francis_henry_grenfell.php
18. McIntosh, Peter C. op. cit. 158
19. Grenfell F H. 'The Scope of Swedish Gymnastics Considered as an Instrument in General Education (Summary)', 243-247, in *Second International Congress on School Hygiene*, 1-391, Transactions, Volume I, The Royal Sanitary Institute, London, 1908.
20. Minute 526/112½, 15 January 1939.

Other References:

Registry of Births
National Probate Calendar
Naval History Home Page
WWI Medals and Honours UK, Naval Medal and Award Rolls, 1793-1972, page 499.
Hadow Report 1928 – Books in Public Elementary Schools
The London Electoral Register-from 1925- 1932.
UK naval Lists
London Gazette Supplement 23 march 1917.
Grenfell History.co.uk/biographies.

APPENDIX XV
BSA ADVERTISEMENT ON RIFLE PRACTICE

APPENDIX XVI
ARTHUR WAKEFIELD CHAPMAN

Arthur Wakefield Chapman was born on 8 August 1849 at Wanstead Manor, Wanstead, Essex. In the 1851 Census his father (1797-1854) was registered as Henry Chapman, aged fifty-two, East India Agent and Merchant. His wife was Priscilla (1808-1887) and she was aged forty when Arthur Wakefield was aged one year. There were four other siblings.

By 1861 his mother was described as a widow with only three of the children registered.

He was married on 7 September 1876 to Agnes Mangles (1850-1906) at St. Paul's Church, Tongham, Surrey, daughter of the late Captain Mangles of Poyle Park, formerly chairman of the South Western Railway Company.

Chapman was a partner in a Calcutta merchant firm but retired to Surrey and became Chairman of the Farnham School Board. He was appointed as a magistrate in Farnham in January 1894.

When the School Boards were abolished by the 1902 Act he was selected as a member of the SEC and became the first chairman of the Elementary Education Sub-Committee in the *First Report of the SEC* dated 12 May 1903 pp. 473-616, 498.

In 1904 he succeeded to the Chair of the Education Committee and continued in that post until 1911, when he became Chair of Surrey County Council, which he held until 1917.

He was knighted in the New Year's Honours List 1915.

> "Chapman was probably the commanding personality of the County Council in the first quarter of the 20th century….. He was a dominating personality. He knew what he wanted and he had the determination to get his own way which enabled him usually to succeed in his proposals…Surrey's advances in education and public health were ascribed to his decidedly progressive views."[1]

He died on 25 March 1926.

Notes

1. Robinson, David, *Surrey Through The Century 1889-1989*, 16, Surrey County Council, 1989. (NB. Robinson was the County Archivist.) A small-framed photograph of Chapman may also be found on page 16 of the book)

APPENDIX XVII
DOROTHY LE COUTEUR 1882-1962

Miss Dorothy Le Couteur was born on the 2 February 1882 in St Helier, Jersey, in the Channel Islands. She died at Farnborough Hospital, Kent, on 12 December 1962. Her address at the time of her death was 101 Leonard Road, Beckenham, Kent. Her estate was valued at £5,670. 1s. 6d.

In the 1891 census she is listed as being nine years of age and living at 9 Gloucester Street, St Helier, Jersey. Her father, a merchant, was Francis Edward Le Couteur and he was aged forty in 1891. He died on 20 March 1920 at the City of London Asylum, Dartford, Kent. Her mother was Alice Jane Le Couteur aged thirty-five. The family consisted of two other daughters and a son.

By 1911 she was living at 3 Ulandi Road, Blackheath, SE London. Her occupation was that of Physical Instructress, and it would appear that her mother and brother Frank lived at the same address. A later address was "Westwood" Burrows Lane, Gomshall, Surrey.

Dorothy was initially appointed in Surrey as Assistant Instructress of PT at an interview held on 19 March 1913. This appointment was a prelude to a distinguished career, which was to span almost thirty years of service to the children of Surrey's schools in the sphere of physical education. She was appointed full-time Organiser of PT on the Surrey County Staff from 1 January 1917 at a salary of £200 under the general supervision of the County Inspector.

In one sense, therefore, she carried on a long tradition of educational service in the field of PE initiated by Major Norman, strengthened by Lt Col Mignon and completed by Dorothy until just after the beginning of the Second World War. This tradition of service to the schools may be found in Log Book entries, which are an indelible memorial to the expertise, exposition and organizational skills of this remarkable trio.

Dorothy had qualified at Madame Bergman Osterberg's Physical Training College in Dartford in 1901. In 1911 she accompanied a fourteen-person party[1] to Switzerland, which included her friend Jane Neave and J R R Tolkien.[2] Dorothy sketched a map of the tour.[3]

Jane, who had an interest in sport,[4] was a science teacher at King Edward's Foundation Bath Row School. She earned an extra £5 a year at the school for taking responsibility for school drill.[5] It is not exactly clear where and when Jane and Dorothy met but they both had an evident and continued interest in education.[6]

Not long after her appointment as Assistant Inspectress with Surrey County Council, the Stepgates School Girls Log Book opened on 15 November 1912, an entry, 15 January 1914, describes her as

"Assistant Inspectress of Drill visited this morning and saw the Morris Dancing of Standards II, III, VI and VII"

It would be speculative to assert that her role was that of encouraging Country and Morris dance. Nevertheless, folk dance had been encouraged by the 1909 Syllabus.

A further entry, 27 March 1914, indicates

"A display in Morris Dancing is to be given in the evening in the School Hall in aid of the Library (fund). This dancing has been taught in the time devoted to physical training, and during the present week, the classes have made use of the Platform. Special times have been arranged for this"

Three days later Captain Mignon and Monsieur Knudsen, Inspector of PT for Denmark visited to watch the Morris dancing and listen to the singing of Old Folk Songs. A subsequent visitor, 31 May 1915, Miss Askman from the Esperance Club in London came to teach Morris and Country Dancing and Folk Songs to the various standards.

It seems clear that local displays in dancing were held to raise funds for the war effort in aid of the Red Cross Military Hospital and the Chertsey Nursing Association. Nor was the raising of funds confined to local charities. On 10 July 1916, the girls and infants combined to give an outdoor display of drills, songs, games and dances in aid of starving Belgium children, which raised £5. 15s. 3d.

It would seem that Dorothy built an affectionate and professional relationship with this school. On 25 January 1926, for example, she visited in connection with the formation of a Folk Dancing Society. On 14 February 1939 she presented the PT Silver Cup to Thames house (Blue) for the highest marks gained for the day and past year. The last entry, relating to her visits, was on 18 July 1939.

The visit of 25 January 1926 seems to have had a direct relationship with the formation of a West Surrey Branch of the English Folk Dance Society in the week prior to that of Saturday 5 December 1925.[7] At the meeting was Douglas Kennedy, the organizing director of the society, who noted that it was not desired to cut across any interest that was currently being carried on. This comment appears to have had some resonance concerning Women's Institutes to which men were not admitted.

The fashion for Jazz also appears to have had some relevance to the formation of the Branch. The committee of the branch consisted of twenty-one members, four of whom were men. Dorothy was third on the list of all the names published.

Saturday, 12 December 1925 was also a busy day for Dorothy.[8] Several villages in East Surrey were represented at the Country Dance Party at the Adult School Hall, Croydon, and, with their enthusiastic and unanimous approval an East Surrey and Croydon Branch of the English Folk Dance Society was formed. According to the newspaper article there were 6,000 members of the Society founded by Cecil Sharp in 1911 and the aim was to raise a sum of £25,000 to secure and equip a building in London, which would not only serve to perpetuate the memory of the founder, but, also to act as as a permanent home of English folk-music and dance. In East Surrey and Croydon £63 had already been raised for the Cecil Sharp Memorial Fund as it was known.

Douglas Kennedy was also at this meeting and a Committee of twelve ladies, among whom was Dorothy, and three men were appointed. Folk Dance was subsequently practiced at many schools within the SEC's jurisdiction.

One of those schools was the Goldsworth School in Woking, where children from the school attended Guildford's Folk Dance Festivals every year from 1928 to 1939. Folk dancing at Guildford seems to have developed from a competition judged merely on Folk Dance up to1930, in which year it became a festival embracing Singing Games, Folk Singing and Folk Dancing. The competitive element remained in all three activities but the change to festival status presumably was a necessary concomitant of these three activities within the schools and gave them a broader-based curriculum.

On 28 March 1928 children from the school aged under ten danced at the competition having to go to school to get their mark and proceeding to Guildford on the 09:15 to Guildford. Out of nineteen teams entering the competition, they came third, scoring 89 out of 100 marks.

The 1929 team scored 88 marks out of 100 and Goldsworth were one mark below the winners. They had to dance "Rufty Tufty, London is a Fine Town and Goddesses". Twenty-four schools entered in that year.

The following year the competition was held on 24 March 1930. Children were entered for all three activities, which were now part of the festival. They came first in the Singing Games and Folk Dance. It would have been a clean sweep except for the fact that they were one point behind the winners in Folk Songs. Twenty-two teams had entered. Honours certificates were awarded in all three activities and they won a shield for the dancing.

Three teams were again entered for the 1931 competition. Again the children left on, this time, the 09:20 train. For the 1932 competition on 8 March only two teams participated. Both teams were awarded 84 marks for the songs and the country dancing.

By 1933 three teams entered and gained 80 marks for Folk Songs, 85 for Singing Games and 82 for the dancing. It would appear that honours certificates were awarded for marks 85 and above.

In 1934 five teams from the school participated in different age categories. All the teams were awarded certificates, three teams gaining honours for marks over 85. The teams were Folk Songs 80 marks, Singing Games 87, under 9s country dancing 82, under 11s country dance 88 and under 11's (girls) 86.

The 1935 team consisted of two Folk Dance teams, one under 9 and one under 11. The former won the first place while the latter gained third place. The team entered for the Folk Song competition but did not figure in the awards.

It would appear that the 1936 competitions were spread over two days The school earned first prize in both Junior Songs and in the under11's mixed dancing. On the following day, 25 March, a boys' sword dance team and a group of infants for Singing Games were despatched. All must have done well since on Saturday, 28 March, fifty children performed at a show given by the winning teams. Six teams entered and all six gained certificates, three gaining first place and one second.

The school was again in top form for the festival of 12 March 1937. Three firsts are recorded in Folk Songs, Girls Sword Dance and Boys Sword Dance. They came second in country dancing with 94 marks and the remaining two teams gained certificates with marks over 80.

Three teams travelled to the competition on 29 March 1938, and 21 March 1939. In the former, the teams consisted of two country dancing teams and one sword dance. In the latter, all three teams received certificates with silver stars.

It is important to stress that dancing, in particular, was being practiced throughout Surrey's Elementary Schools. At the 1931 competition, which, according to the West Clandon School's Log Books took place on 17 and 18 March (p. 361), the children of West Clandon came third with 82 marks in Class 7 of the competition and third also with a mixed team, 80 marks in Class 6 of the competition.

Competition wasn't the only motivation for embracing Country Dance into Surrey's Elementary Schools for Sir Arthur Robert Glyn (1870-1942), a member of the SEC, held Country Dance parties at his home in Ewell. Children from West Clandon attended one of these on 19 June 1935 (p. 397) and also on 19 June 1940. These parties appear to have been fairly extensive in their sweep of the geography of Surrey as eight girls from Stepgates School attended one of these on 6 July 1938, which took place between 16:30 to 18:30.

Dorothy's initial duties at Surrey may be said to have encompassed "seeing" the drill and games of both infant and older scholars as at West Clandon on 23 October 1913.

These inspection visits had been a visible part of the inspection process since the appointment of Major Norman. His assistant, Sergeant Mills, had also been a visible presence in Surrey's Elementary Schools. In this, he appears to have followed up on the visits of Norman and Mignon in order to supplement their work of teacher training in the art of teaching Swedish Drill to the scholars in their charge.

Between 1903 and 17 November 1911 Sergeant Mills is recorded in the Goldsworth Log Books of visiting the school five times in a follow-up capacity. Even prior to the appointment of Major Norman, a visit on 10 July 1903 to the school by Colonel Fox and Lord Londonderry suggests the school already carried a high profile in educational terms. In this respect Lieutenant Commander F H Grenfell, who had replaced Colonel Fox as Chief Inspector of PT at the Board of Education, visited the school on 7 July, 1911.

Dorothy first visited the school on 26 June 1914. According to Log book entries further visits were made on 24 February 1922, 8 March 1928, 11 May 1928, 11 April 1930, 6 December 1933, 12 September 1935, and 5 May 1936. On the face of it this doesn't seem very many but when it is considered that she had 270 elementary schools and a number of secondary schools in her charge it displays a high degree of supervision especially in an age where most transport was by train.

Two events of special importance are recorded in the Log Books. On 11 May 1928, Dorothy brought Miss N M Palmer, a PE Inspector at the Board of Education to see the physical work in the top form. This visit suggests a high standard of achievement in the physical work of the school. That the standards were not only high but sustained is manifested by a Log Book entry of 20 February 1935. The entry states that a team of children, twenty boys and twenty girls, were asked by the County Organiser, Dorothy, to give a demonstration of a twenty-minute lesson on 1 March 1935 at a meeting of the National Association of Organisers of Physical Education at Chelsea. On 15 March 1935 Dorothy brought Haig-Brown, the Surrey Schools Inspector to "see" the Chelsea children.

When Dorothy was first appointed she was clearly aware that much work had been done to establish swimming by Major Norman, and, the then Captain Mignon and the development of swimming in Surrey's Public Elementary Schools is mapped out by J R Pegg in the *In The Swim: The Origins and Systematic Development of Children's Swimming in the County of Surrey's Public Elementary Schools 1905-1921 Pioneered by Major Arthur Ormand Norman: A Documentary History, with Various Appendices Including Swimming and Washing Verminous Children in the London School Board*, 2016.

Yet that wasn't the end of the story. An entry in the West Clandon School's Log Book of 17 June 1919 notes that twelve boys started a course of swimming lessons at Guildford Baths. 'The boys leave school at 15:00 hours, while the girls began on Friday morning leaving school at 11:00. The afternoon session on Friday during the swimming course will begin at 14:00 hours to enable the girls to return in time.'

Swimming seems to have resumed at various intervals, for example see the entry of 15 July 1925, nevertheless, it doesn't necessarily mean that all had been plain sailing. On 10 May 1928, Dorothy called to discuss the swimming class but only one boy was willing to join. The girls were very keen but there was "no opportunity for them". This doesn't quite square with previous entries, but, whatever the problem, there seems to have been some kind of re-evaluation, for by 18 April 1929, Dorothy called in to enquire about the possibility of children from Clandon going to Effingham for swimming lessons. This seems to have become established procedure, since on 19 June 1935,

"15 children attended swimming in the Effingham baths this morning"

On the morning of 25 September 1935, fifteen children attended the final session of the season in the Effingham baths. Five certificates were awarded for swimming a length at which Dorothy was present.

It has always to be borne in mind that the problem of girls learning to swim prior to the Second World War was of a different gender dimension to the morays of today. Instructors for girls were difficult to recruit partly because the location of some of the swimming places was often in rivers, lakes and ponds especially in the earlier part of the 20th century. If this incident is frustratingly incomplete it is also an indication of Dorothy's ability to smooth over problems in a diplomatic manner. One of the greatest accolades that Dorothy received was in the early 1930s when she became Principal of Dartford College for a term.

Her appointment was a result of a *Special Meeting of the Committee of Management held at the Ministry of Health* on Friday 28 February 1930. Present at the meeting was Sir George Newman (Chair), Dame Janet Campbell, Captain Grenfell, Mrs Hatfield, Dr Lambert, Miss Lloyd Evans, Miss Sandord and Sir Amherst Selby-Bigge.

Newman was the CMO at the Board of Education and the Ministry of Health, Janet Campbell was his deputy, Grenfell was the Chief Inspector of Physical Training and Selby-Bigge was the permanent secretary at the Board.

The reason for the meeting was a deputation received from the Head Mistresses Association consisting of Miss Addison Phillips, MA, President (Clifton High School), Dr Lowe (Leeds Girls' High School), Miss Sparks Ladies College Cheltenham), Miss Strudwick (St Paul's Girls' School), Miss de Zouche (Girls' High School, Wolverhampton), Miss Young (Secretary).

The testimony of Miss Phillips referred to the deputation's deep concern at the unrest, which they believed to have existed at Dartford College during the previous two years. The understanding was that the Bergman Osterberg Union was dissatisfied with the management of the College. In fifteen years there had been four Principals. Four members of staff had resigned on a question of principle. The deputation was aware that the Committee had not exceeded their statutory powers but felt that the position of the Principal had not always been in accordance with her expectations. Specific instances were:

1. The dismissal of Miss Cranfield without consulting the Principal.
2. Miss Spalding's present position which had also been arranged without the concurrence of the Principal.
3. The recent appointment of two mistresses (Miss Dewey and Miss McLaren) which were made without consulting the Principal.
4. The admission of an unnamed student in spite of a protest by her head mistress.
5. Reports by HMI, which, it was implied, were biased and which had resulted in re-organisation and changes in the staff contrary to the wishes of the Principal.
6. The failure to advertise vacancies at the College.

These points were replied to in detail by the Chairman and other members of the Committee who assured the deputation that the Committee were only too anxious to give the Principal the support that she desired to have. It was, however, necessary to maintain a high standard of technical performance to the work of the College as well as sustain a satisfactory standard of social and moral government of the College.

Further discussion followed with the head mistresses apparently acknowledging that they had been gravely misinformed regarding the six points raised.

Two points were subsequently accepted as a necessary condition of the Principal's powers:

- A. that the Principal should be adequately consulted regarding staff appointments
- B. that the Principal should be responsible to the Committee of Management for the discipline and internal organization of the College.

The Committee assured the deputation that it entirely agreed with these points and this had been their practice in the past and would be so in the future.

Sir George Newman suggested that it was desirable to make temporary arrangements for the summer term and considerations of a more permanent appointment be made at a later date. His suggestion was that the temporary appointment of an HMI would be appropriate but Sir Amherst Selby-Bigge emphasised that the Board of Education would be reluctant to support such an appointment. Sir George suggested that the Honorary Secretary should approach Dorothy Le Couteur and invite her to accept the position for the summer term provided Surrey County Council was prepared to release her. This was agreed. Subsequently, Dorothy filled the vacancy in a temporary capacity for the summer term.

The suggestion from the staff at the BOU archive catalogue was that Dorothy was invited to be Principal on the suggestion of Sir George on the basis of his previous knowledge of her work and was assured of her ability to deal with unrest among staff and students resulting from the resignation of Miss Lett, the then Principal, in December 1929 and other key members of staff on a question of principle.

Photograph by kind permission from the collection of Andrew Morton
From the book Tolkien's Gedling by Andrew H. Morton and John Hayes, page 70
Dorothy Le Couteur is third from the left.

*Photograph by kind permission from the collection of Andrew Morton
From the book Tolkien's Gedling by Andrew H. Morton and John Hayes,
Photograph page XII after page 48 "The school inspector Dorothy Le Couteur is between
Colin's two sisters"*

*Sir George Newman and Miss Le Couteur on Parents Day 1930
Photograph courtesy of the Bergman Osterberg Union Archive, North West Kent College,
Dartford, Kent*

Notes
1. Morton, Andrew H and Hayes, John, *Tolkien's Gedling*, 48, Brewin Books, Studley, Warwickshire, B80 7HP, 2008
2. Ibid., 6
3. Ibid., 71
4. Ibid., 12
5. Ibid.
6. Ibid., 13
7. *The Surrey Advertiser and County Times*, Saturday, 5 December 1925, 7.
8. *Surrey Mirror and County Post*, Friday 18 December 1925, 5.

Other Sources
Registry of Births
England and Wales National Probate Calendar (Index of wills and and Administration
Channel Island Census 1881

English Census 1991
The Log Books of Stepgates School, Chertsey, Surrey
The Log Books of Goldsworth School, Woking, Surrey
The Log Books of West Clandon School, West Clandon, Surrey
Bergman Osterberg Trust, by kind permission of Rosemary Moon at the Bergman Osterberg Union (BOU) Archive

APPENDIX XVIII
SCC MANAGERS' HANDBOOK 1912 - THE PT CURRICULUM

When Dorothy was appointed as Assistant Physical Training Instructress in 1913 she had the *Handbook for Managers of PES*, 75-93, Second Edition, SCC, 1-243, 1912 as a guide. Chapter VII spells out the curriculum of an Elementary School and at page 65, Section 9(e) the heading is entitled 'Physical Training and the Laws of Health'.

The curriculum of an Elementary School must include, in addition to instruction in the simple laws of health, a systematic course of physical training.

"The Committee has adopted the Syllabus of Physical Training for Elementary Schools published by the Board of Education, 1909, subject to certain minor modifications, and have decided that the teaching of this Syllabus shall be given in all schools under their jurisdiction and that it shall be given by School Teachers.

Arrangements have been made by the Committee whereby they can attend classes of instruction in this subject held by the Superintendent of PT.

The object of PT is of a two-fold character
(a) Physical, i.e. to maintain, and, if possible, improve the health and physique of the child
(b) Educational, i.e. to develop in the scholars qualities of alertness, decision concentration and self-control

The Syllabus is designed
(a) To bring about *Uniformity*, for the purpose of avoiding the waste of time and energy incidental to the transference of pupils and teachers from one school district to another
(b) To ensure that the exercises taught shall not be harmful to the most delicate of children. PT in Elementary Schools has nothing to do with militarism; it is not designed for the purpose of producing soldiers or athletes, but to rear a healthy race of men and women, who shall be able to enjoy a happy and useful life.

Children in rural districts require it quite as much as children in the towns. If a system of PT is to produce good results it must be
(a) *Systematic* because organised method produces far better results than spasmodic and disjointed efforts
(b) *Gradual* avoid danger to the heart, lungs and other internal organs
(c) *Progressive* because it is only by the reaction of muscle upon nerve-each helping the other-that any improvement can or does take place
(d) *Continuous* because of the rapid loss of "good condition" by periods of inactivity

Whenever practicable, exercises should be performed in the open air, the interval being used to obtain a thorough ventilation of the school premises, and, particularly the classrooms, which, as a rule, suffer most in this respect.

Ample playground space is required for children's games which really form an integral part of the course of physical exercises. Inasmuch as the effect of physical exercises depends, in no small measure upon their regularity, and, as the climate of this country is that exercises in the open air must constantly be suspended, the provision of play sheds or rooms for physical exercises, other than the ordinary classroom, should be considered as an almost indispensable part of the school equipment.

Organised games are closely allied to PT and their importance as an educational factor should be fully recognised. The Committee's regulations as to the provision of apparatus for this purpose may be found in Chapter IX.

Managers of schools should neglect no opportunity of utilizing to the full the interest and activity of voluntary helpers, who, in this department of school work, more than in any other, have it in their power to render services of the most voluntary kind.

Managers should also endeavour to enlist the interest and sympathy of football, cricket or hockey clubs, and of owners of swimming baths, who may be disposed to place part of their grounds or baths at the disposal of schools when the grounds are not being used otherwise.

Swimming

Every encouragement should be given to the teaching of *Swimming* especially where public baths are available for the purpose, and life-saving lessons should be given at the same time. Swimming may be entered in the approved Time-Table and counted as attendance. The Committee will be glad to cooperate with Managers in obtaining favourable terms for the attendance if children from Elementary Schools at swimming baths, provided it is under proper control and supervision.

Equipment – Chapter 9 page 93
    (d)   Organised Games

The Committee will sanction the supply of apparatus for organised games when requisitioned by the Managers subject to the following conditions:
- (1) That the games are included in the School Time-Table under article 44(f) of the Code
- (2) That the apparatus is used solely during the hours fixed by the Time-table for such instruction
- (3) That such apparatus can be provided within the estimated amount allowed for books, stationery and apparatus without unduly curtailing the supply of essentials."

APPENDIX XIX
ELEMENTARY EDUCATION IN SURREY 1903

"Modern Education in Surrey can be said to have begun when
the new County Council established a Technical Instruction
Committee in 1891 – "[1]

The 1902 Act established Lea(s), which, in Surrey's case, was the SEC.[2] The appointed day was 1 April 1903.[3] The Elementary Education Sub-Committee had met on four occasions prior to the *1st Report of the SEC* on 12 May 1903: 24 and 31 March and 7 and 20 April 1903. A W Chapman was elected chairman.

The SEC was now responsible for:

65	Council Schools	(formerly under the control of Board Schools)
177	Voluntary Schools	Church of England (C of E)* British, (i.e. non-conformist) Roman Catholic (RC)
4	Schools	attached to Institutes
246		

*Some of the Church of England Schools were in fact *National* Schools because they were schools still in union with the *National Society for Promoting the Education of the Poor in the Principles of the Established Church* founded in 1811. British Schools were associated with the *The British and Foreign School Society* founded in 1808. National schools followed the Bell system and British schools the Lancaster system of monitorial schooling. In 1906 these distinctions were abolished. *See* the *Report of the Board of Education for 1906-1907*, Command 3862, p. 28.

In addition two voluntary schools were applying to become PES; Cobham Downside and Godstone Felbridge. Two voluntary schools has also applied to become Council schools, Warbridge (C of E) and Weybridge Oatlands (British).[4]

Richmond was applying to become a Part III authority.[5]

The implementation of the 1902 Act meant that the SEC had the powers to control a number of School Boards. On 31 March 2003 the following School Boards were incorporated into the SEC:[6]

Board	Date of Formation	No. of Schools	Population
North West Division			
Pyrford	19-12-1891	1	528
Windlesham	16-12-1871	2	3,415
Frimley	08-09-1883	2	8,409

Bisley	11-03-1893	-	747
Egham	04-07-1884	3	11,895
Woking	30-04-1874	7	16,244
Pirbright	01-04-1885	1	1,540
Walton-on-Thames	02-09-1878	4	10,329
South West Division			
Farnham	24-04-1883	5	14,582
Worplesdon	05-06-1882	2	1,843
Guildford	02-04-1883	5	15,943
Stoke-next-Guildford			4,462
Shalford	14-02-1881	1	2,082
Alford	24-06-1874	1	517
North Central Division			
West Molesley	04-10-1879	1	915
Thames Ditton	09-04-1881	2	4,986
Central Division			
Banstead and	28-04-1874	1	5,624
Kingswood		2	754
Sutton	19-03-1874	4	17,223
Northern Division			
Barnes	04-06-1878	4	10,047
North East Division			
Mitcham	24-02-1871	4	14,903
Mid-Eastern Division			
Carshalton	15-04-1873	1	6,746
South East Division			
Caterham	09-12-1871	2	9,486
Warlingham	30-04-1872	2	2,573
Sanderstead	15-01-1875	1	1,001
Southern Division			
Betchworth	17-07-1877	2	1,789
Merstham	06-09-1889	1	2,015
Bletchingley	29-11-1873	1	2,128
Horley	09-11-1872	3	4,133
Burstow with Bletchingley and Nutfield Contributaries	23-07-1874	2	1,860
Lingfield	25-09-1880	3	3,718

The Boards at Pyrford, Bisley, Egham, Walton-on-Thames, West Molesley, Banstead and Kingswood, Barnes, Sanderstead, Bletchingley and Burstow were formed compulsorily under Section 10 or Section 40 of the Elementary Education Act 1870.

The Boards at Frimley, Pirbright, Worplesdon, Farnham District and Thames Ditton were formed under Section 12 (2).

This total adds up to 70. (The Guildford Schools seem to have been included in this total, although it is not altogether clear why.)

Note: This appendix may also be found as Chapter 2 of the book relating to *In Sickness and In Health: The Origins and Systematic Development of Children's Medical Inspection and Treatment in the County of Surrey's Public Elementary Schools 1905-1921 Pioneered by Dr Thomas Henry Jones, A Documentary History*, Volume 1 by J Robert Pegg.

Notes

1. Manning, F E, ed. *Surrey Past and Present*, 113, SCC, 1971.
2. SHC, Report of the Elementary Education Sub-Committee, (REES), 498-495, the sub-committee met 24 March 1903; 31 March 1903; 7 April 1903; 20 April 1903 in *1st Report of the SEC*, 12 May 1903, 473-616.
3. SHC, ibid., Appendix K, 536.
4. Ibid., REES, 498, ibid.
5. Ibid.
6. Ibid., Appendix G, 529-531.

BIBLIOGRAPHY

Acts of Parliament

The Elementary Education Act, 1870, 33 and 34 Vict., c. 75

The Elementary Education (Blind and Deaf Children) Act 1893, 56 and 57 Vict., c. 42

Elementary Education (Defective and Epileptic Children) Act 1899, 62 and 63 Vict., c. 32

The Education Act 1902, 2 Edw. VII, c.42

Education (Provision of Meals) Act 1906, 6 Edw. VII, c. 57

Education (Administrative Provisions) Act 1907, 7 Edw. VII, c. 43

Education (Provision of Meals) Act 1914, 4 &5 Geo V c. 20

Education Act 1918, 8 & 9 Geo V c. 39

Education Act 1921, 11 & 12 Geo c. 51

Parliamentary Papers

PP 1861 Volume XXI, Royal Commission to Enquire into the Present State of Popular Education in England, and to Consider and Report what Measures, if, any are required for the Extension of Sound and Cheap Elementary Instruction to all classes of the People.

PP 1862 Volume XLIII, Accounts and Papers, Copy of Two Papers submitted to the (Newcastle) Commisssion by Mr Chadwick, one entitled Communications on Half-Time Teaching and on Military Drills, the other a letter to Mr Senior explanatory of the former paper. Printed 21 March 1862.

PP 1871 Command 252, volume lv, 303, Minute of the Right Honourable The Lords of the Committee of the Privy Council on Education establishing A New Code of Regulations 1871

PP 1875 lxiv, New Code of Regulations with an appendix of New Articles and of all articles modified by the Right Honourable the Lords of the Committee of the Privy Council on Education, Article 24.

PP 1882 Command 3152, 1, 511, Minute of the 6th March 1882, establishing a New Code of regulations by the Right Honourable The Lords of the Committee of the Privy Council on Education.

PP 1884 lxi, 293, Report of Dr Crichton-Browne on Overpressure and the Response in the Memorandum by Mr J G Fitch..

PP 1901 Command 513, LV, 743, Code of Regulations for day Schools with Schedules and Appendices.

PP 1903 Command 1507, xxx, 1, Report of the Royal Commission on Physical Training (Scotland), Volume 1, Report and Appendix.

PP 1903 Command 1508, xxx, 123, Report of the Royal Commission on Physical Training (Scotland), Volume II, Minutes of Evidence and Index.

PP 1904 Command 2032, xix, 411, Report of the Inter-Departmental Committee on the Model Course of Physical Exercises.

PP 1904 Command 2175, xxxii, 1, Report of the Inter-Departmental Committee on Physical Deterioration, Volume I, Report and Index.

PP 1904 Command 2210, xxxii, 145, Minutes of Evidence taken before the Inter-Departmental Committee on Physical Deterioration, List of Witnesses and Minutes of Evidence.

PP 1906 Command 2779, xlvii, 1, Report and Appendices of the Inter-Departmental Committee on MI and Feeding of Children attending Public Elementary Schools.

PP 1906 Command 2784, xlvii, 157, List of Witnesses, Evidence, Appendices and Index of the Inter-Departmental Committee on MI and Feeding of Children attending Public Elementary Schools.

Education Department

1882 New Code of Regulations, Instructions to HM Inspectors, England and Wales, d. 9 August 1882.

1890 Minute of the 10 March 1890 establishing a New Code of Regulations, Article 101b A Grant for Discipline and Organisation of 1/- or 1/6 (one shilling and sixpence).

1893 General Report for the year 1893 by the Reverend T.W. Sharpe, C.B., Her Majesty's Senior Chief Inspector, on the Schools in the Metropolitan Division, comprising the School Board for London, the County of Middlesex and part of Essex, pp. 89-114 in Report of the Committee of Council on Education (England and Wales 1893/4)

1894 Code of Regulations for Day Schools with Schedules and Appendices

1901 Memorandum of the Departmental Committee on Training College Courses of Instruction, Volume I, evidence of J C Colvill.

Board of Education

1902 A Model Course of Physical Training for Use in the Upper Departments of Public Elementary Schools.

1902 Memorandum on Physical Training. Practical Suggestions Principally for Rural Schools.

1904 Circular 515 d. 22 August 1904, Syllabus of Physical Exercises for use in Public Elementary Schools

1905 Handbook of Suggestions for the Use of Teachers and Others concerned in the work of Public Elementary Schools.

1905 Syllabus of Physical Exercises for use in Public Elementary Schools

1906 Code of Regulations for Public Elementary Schools with Schedules, Article 44f Preface, VI.

1907 Circular 552, 1 January 1907 (Provision of Meals).

1907 Code of Regulations for Public Elementary Schools.

1909 The Syllabus of Physical Exercises for Public Elementary Schools.

1909 Circular 727, No Title, d. September 1909.

1912 Report of the Departmental Committee appointed to inquire into Certain Questions In Connexion With The Playgrounds of Public Elementary Schools with Abstracts of Evidence.

1917 Circular 976 d. 10 February 1917, Grants in Aid of the Organization and Supervision of the Teaching of PT in Public Elementary Schools.

1918 Circular 1029 d. 16 February 1918, to Local Eucation Authorities employing Women Organisers of Physical Training.

1919 Circular 1138 d. 12 December 1919, Revised Syllabus of Physical Exercises to Local Education Authorities.

1931 Report of the Consultative Committee of the Board of Education on the Primary School

The National Archives

Ed.22/9 The Teaching of Dancing Steps and Exercises to Scholars in Public Elementary Schools, Memo to Inspectors, E. No. 39, 24 July 1909, 1-2.

Ed.23/198 Letter d. 4 February 1903; Letter d. 3 July 1903

Ed.24/37A A Report of the Physical Training Committee

Ed.142/39 Circular 452, d. 20 June 1901, A Model Course of Physical Training for Use in the Upper Departments of Public Elementary Schools, (mentioned) in the Day School Code, Schedule III (This Circular refers to the version of the Model Course which is the non-picture version)

HO 140/22 A Calendar of Prisoners Tried at Assizes & Quarter Sessions, Winter Gaol delivery 1873

WO/32/6209 Parkes E A, MD, FRS, Appendix A Memo by Dr Parkes in Hammersley F, et al., Report of the Committee appointed to Report on Gymnastic Instruction for the Army, 1864.

Surrey History Centre

Please Note: At least two versions of the printed Surrey Education Minutes, each with different page number systems, exist or have existed.

Surrey Education Committee Reports

8th Report of the SEC d. 8 November 1904
10th Report of the SEC d. 9 May 1905
11th Report of the SEC d. 25 July 1905
12th Report of the SEC d. 14 November 1905
13th Report of the SEC d. 13 February 1906
15th Report of the SEC d. 8 May 1906
16th Report of the SEC d. 31 July 1906
17th Report of the SEC d. 13 November 1906.
18th Report of the SEC d. 12 February 1907
19th Report of the SEC d. 14 May 1907
20th Report of the SEC d. 30 July 1907
21st Report of the SEC d. 12 November 1907
22nd Report of the SEC d. 11 February 1908
23rd Report of the SEC d. 12 May 1908
24th Report of the SEC d. 28 July 1908
25th Report of the SEC d. 10 November 1908
26th Report of the SEC d. 12 January 1909
27th Report of the SEC d. 16 March 1909
28th Report of the SEC d. 11 May 1909
31st Report of the SEC d. 11 January 1910
32nd Report of the SEC d. 15 March 1910
33rd Report of the SEC d. 10 May 1910
34th Report of the SEC d. 26 July 1910
35th Report of the SEC d. 8 November 1910
36th Report of the SEC d. 10 January 1911
37th Report of the SEC d. 14 March 1911

40th Report of the SEC d. 14 November 1911
41st Report of the SEC d. 9 January 1912
45th Report of the SEC d. 12 November 1912
47th Report of the SEC d. 11 March 1913
48th Report of the SEC d. 22 May 1913
66th Report of the SEC d. 9 January 1917
68th Report of the SEC d. 31 July 1917

Surrey Quarter Sessions d. 13 November 1906

Log Books
C/ES/115/2/1/1 Log Book Dorking British School, 261
Log Book of Goldsworth School, Woking.
Log Books of Stepgates School Chertsey, Surrey.

Hansard

Hansard, House of Commons, Fourth Series, Volume CXX, 25 March 1903.

Hansard, House of Lords, Fourth Series, Volume CXXIV, 6 July 1903. (Lord Meath, The National Standard of Physical Health)

Hansard, House of Lords, Volume II, National Service (Training and Home Defence) Bill, d.12 July 1909, column 329.

Hansard, House of Commons, Fourth Series, Volume 125, Commons Questions, 15 July 1903.

Unpublished Ph. D. Theses

May, J., Curriculum Development Under the School Board for London,
Physical Education, 1971, University of Leicester

Other Theses

Ashley, Roy, A Study in the Teaching of Physical Education in Elementary Schools in England and Wales 1890-1918, M. Ed. Thesis, Liverpool, 1967

Wrap.warwick.ac.uk/57590/1/wrap
Greenslade, William Paul, MA. The Concept of Degeneration 1880-1910 with Particular Reference t the Work of Thomas Hardy, George Gissing and H G Wells. A Thesis submitted for the degree of Doctor of Philosophy in the University of Warwick, 1-455, September 1982

Articles

British Medical Journal, 18 July 1903; 14 September 1903.

Grenfell, F H. The Scope of Swedish Gymnastics Considered as an Instrument in *General Education in Transactions of the Second International Congress on School Hygiene.*

Physical Degeneration in the *British Medical Journal*, 5 December 1903.

The Fitness of the Nation-Physical and Health Education in *The 19th and 20th Centuries-History of Education Society Conference Papers* (December 1982)

MacMillans Magazine, No. 58 Volume X, August 1864.

Maurice, Major-General Sir Frederick, (pseudonym Miles), Where To Get Men in *The Contemporary Review*, Volume LXXXIII, 1903.

Maurice, Major-General Sir Frederick, National Health: A Soldier's Study in *The Contemporary Review*, Volume LXXXIII, 1903.

Meath, Earl of, *Universal Military Training for Lads in the Nineteenth Century and After*, Volume LVII, January-June 1905.

Meath, Earl of, Decay of Bodily Strength in Towns in *The Nineteenth Century*, Volume XXI, January-June, 1897.

Meath, Earl of, Correspondence, Sir Henry Havelock Allen and His Scheme for Training To Arms The Youth of the Nation in *The Fortnightly Review*, Volume LXI, 1897.

Meath, Earl of. *Health and Physique of our City Populations*, Reprinted by permission from The Nineteenth Century, July 1881 in Meath, Earl of, Edited, *Prosperity or Pauperism, Physical, Industrial and Technical Training*, Longmans, Green and Co., London, 1888.

Springhall John O. Lord Meath, Youth and Empire in *The Journal of Contemporary History*, Volume 5 No 4, 1978.

An Impeachment of the National Health in *The Lancet*, 1903.

The Lancet, 31 January 1903; 14 February 1903; 11 July 1903; 18 July 1903; 25 July 1903; 6 August 1904; 13 August 1904; 20 August 1904; 10 September, 1904; 12 November 1904

Newspapers

Aldershot Military Gazette, 16 November 1864

Hull Daily Mail, 21 July 1897

Kent & Sussex Courier, 22 March 1918

Portsmouth Evening News, 15 March 1883

The Army and Navy Gazette, 29 August 1908; 29 July 1916; 13 April 1918

The Caledonian Mercury, 25 December 1863; 11 January 1864; 12 June 1865

The Hampshire Advertiser, 12 November 1873

The Inverness Courier, 31 December 1863

The Isle of Wight Observer, 20 December 1873

The Manchester Guardian, 27 April 1903; 23 July 1903

The Morning Post, 10 June 1871; 7 August 1875

The Oxford Chronicle, 4 February 1882

The School Board Chronicle, 15 December 1894, Vol. LII, pp. 702; 30 August 1902, Volume LXVIII, pp. 214-215

The Sheffield Telegraph, 24 June 1910

The Times, 4 January 1902; 7 January 1902; 9 June 1902; 23 July 1902; 16 August 1902; 23 August 1904; 17 November 1904; 8 September 1909; 22 February 1915; 7 August 1916; 13 March 1918; 12 October 1929

The Surrey Times, 29 June 1901; 21 June 1902; 8 July 1905; 22 August 1905; 29 August 1908; 30 July 1910; 28 July 1916

The Times Educational Supplement, 7 December 1915

Vanity Fair, 3 September 1896

Other Sources-On Line

Canada British Regimental Registers of Service 1756-1900

Channel Islands Census 1881

England & Wales National Probate Calendar 1858-1966

English Census 1851-1861-1871-1881-1891-1901-1911

GrenfellHistory.co.uk/biographies

International War Graves Record Added 23 November 2005

London Gazette Supplement 23 March 1917

Museums- The Black Watch Castle Museum Perth Scotland

Naval History-Home Page

Registry of Births Marriages and Deaths

The London Electoral Register 1925-1937

UK Naval Lists

UK Commonwealth War Graves 1914-1921

WW1 Medals & Honours UK, Naval Medal & Award Rolls 1793-1972

Secondary Sources

Aldrich, Richard and Gordon, Peter. *Dictionary of British Educationists*, Woburn Press, London 1989.

Anderson, M S. *The Ascendancy of Europe 1815-1914*, 1972, Pearson Education Limited, Edinburgh, 3rd Edition 2003.

Atkins, J B. *National Physical Training, An Open Debate*, Ibister & Co., London 1904.

Barth, Karl. *From Rousseau to Ritschl*, SCM Press Ltd (English Edition) London, 1959.

Birchenough, Charles. *History of Elementary Education in England and Wales from 1800 to the present day*, University Tutorial Press LD, 3rd Edition, London 1938.

Blaikie, William. *Sound Bodies for Our Boys and Girls*, Sampson Low, Marston, Searle & Rivington, London 1884.

Bramwell, R D. *Elementary School Work 1900-1925*, Institute of Education, Durham 1961.

Brunton, Lauder, Progress of Proposed National League For Physical Education and Improvement in Brunton, Lauder, Sir, *Collected Papers on Physical and Military Training*, Privately Published, London, 1915.

Cassirer, Ernst. Gay, Peter, translated and edited, *The Question of Jean-Jacques Rousseau*, Indiana University Press, 1954. Midland Book Edition, Columbia University Press, 1963.

Chesterton, Thomas. *The Theory of Physical Education in Elementary Schools*, Gale & Polden, London & Aldershot 1895.

Cicero. Translated Keyes, Clinton Walker, *De Legibus*, 52 BC, Book III, Loeb Classical Library No. 213, William Heinnemann, London, 1928.

Cole, Lieutenant-Colonel Howard N. OBE, TD. *The Story of Aldershot, A History and Guide to the Town and Camp*, Gale & Polden, Aldershot, 1911.

Collins, Phillip, *Dickens and Education*, MacMillan & Co Ltd., 1963.

Cross R C and Woozley A D, *Plato's Republic*, Macmillan, St. Martin's Press, London, 1964.

Cunningham, D. *Callisthenics and Drilling Simplified for Schools and Families*, Haughton & Co., London 1875

Curtis, S J and Boultwood M E A. *An Introductory History of English Education since 1800*, 1960, University Tutorial Press Ltd., 4th Edition 1966, London 1966.

Drury, J F W. *Drury's Manual of Education*, John Heywood, Manchester 1903.

Ensor, R C K, *England 1870-1914*, The Clarendon Press, Oxford, 1936.

Eyler, John M, *Victorian Social Medicine*, John Hopkins University Press, Baltimore, 1979.

Fee, Elizabeth and Acheson, Roy, eds. *A History of Education in Public Health*, OUP, 1991.

Floud, Roderick, Wachter, Kenneth and Gregory, Annabel. *Height, Health and History*, CUP, 1990.

Foucault, Michel. *Discipline and Punish, The Birth of the Prison*, Penguin Books, Harmondsworth, Middlesex, 1975, Peregrine Books, 1977.

Foucault, Michel. *The History of Sexuality*, Penguin Books, Harmondsworth, 1987.

Freeden, Michael. *Liberal Languages*, Princeton University Press, Princeton, New Jersey, 2005.

Freeman, Kenneth J. *Schools of Hellas, An Essay on the Practice and Theory of Greek Education from 600 to 300 BC.* Third Edn. Ed. M J Rendall. Macmillan and Co. Ltd, London, 1922.

Frow, Edmund and Ruth. *A Survey of the Half-Time System In Education*, E J Morton, Didsbury, Manchester, 1970.

Galen. *Selected Works, To Thrasyboulos: is healthiness a part of medicine or gymnastics?* Translated with an Introduction and Notes by Singer P N, The World's Classics, OUP, 1997.

Gardner, Brian. *Up The Line To Death, The War Poets 1914-1918*, Methuen, London, 2007.

Gollwitzer, Heinz. *Europe In The Age Of Imperialism 1880-1914*, Thames and Hudson, London 1969.

Gordon, Peter and Lawton, Denis. *Curriculum Change in the Nineteenth and Twentieth Centuries*, Hodder and Stoughton, 1978.

Gordon, Peter and Lawton, Denis. *Dictionary of British Education*, Woburn Press, London 2003.

Grant, John, ed. *Surrey, Historical, Biographical and Pictorial*, The London and Provincial Publishing Company Limited, 84 Hatton Gardens, London. Published only for subscribers.

Greengarten, I M. *Thomas Hill Green and the Development of Liberal-Democratic Thought*. University of Toronto Press, 1981.

Greenslade, William. *Degeneration, Culture and the Novel 1880-1940*, CUP, 1994.

GutsMuths, J C F. *Gymnastics for Youth*, printed for J Johnson, 1800.

Harris, Bernard. *The Health of the Schoolchild, A History of the school medical service in England and Wales*, Open University Press, Buckingham 1995.

Heater, Derek, *Citizenship: The Civic Ideal in World History, Politics and Education.* Picador, London, 2009.

Hodgkinson, Ruth G. *The Origins of the National Health Service, The Medical Services of the New Poor Law 1834-1871*, The Wellcome Historical Medical Library, 1967.

Holmes, Edmond. W*hat Is and What Might Be, A Study of Education in General and Elementary Education in Particular*, Constable & Co. Ltd., London 1912.

Johnstone, J C. Physical Training In The Army And Its Influence On British Schools in McNair, David and Parry, Nicholas A. eds. *Readings in the History of Physical Education*, Auflage, Ahrensburg 1981.

Jones, Greta. *Social Darwinism and English Thought, The Interaction between Biological and Social Theory*, The Harvester Press Limited, Brighton, Sussex, England, 1980.

Jones, W T. *Masters of Political Thought, Machiavelli to Bentham*, George G Harrap & Co Ltd, 1942.

Jordan, Thomas E. *The Degeneracy Crisis and Victorian Youth*, State University of New York Press, Albany, New York, 1993.

Juvenal: Green, Peter. translated. *The Sixteen Satires*, 104 AD, Penguin Harmondsworth, 1967.

Kelly, D V. *39 Months with the "Tigers" 1915-1918.* Ernst Benn Limited, London, 1933 reprinted in The Naval and Military Press Ltd, ND.

Kipling, Rudyard. *The Complete Verse*, 1990, Kyle Cathie Edition, London 2006.

Ledger, Sally and Luckhurst, Roger, eds. *The Fin De Siecle, A Reader in Cultural History c. 1880-1900*, OUP, 2000.

Lee, Stephen J. *Imperial Germany 1871-1918*, Routledge, London 1999.

Leonard, Fred Eugene. *A Guide to the History of Physical Education*, Greenwood Press, Connecticut, Third Edition Revised & Enlarged, 1971.

Lewis, J. *School Drill*, J Lewis, London, 1907.

McIntosh, Peter. *Physical Education in England since 1800*, 1952, Revised & Enlarged Edition, Bell & Hyman Ltd., London 1968.

Mallon, Bill and Buchanan, Ian. *The Olympic Games: Results for all Competitors and All Events with Commentary*, McFarland 2000, Scarecrow Press, Inc., Lanham, USA.

Manning, F E. Ed. *Surrey Past and Present*. SEC, 1971.

Marriott, J A R. *A History of Europe from 1815 to 1939*. Methuen & Co., 5th Edn, London, 1948.

Maudsley, Henry. *Body and Will*, Kegan Paul, Trench & Co., London, 1883.

Meath, Earl of. ed. *Prosperity or Pauperism, Physical, Industrial and Technical Training*, Longmans, Green & Co., London, 1888.

Montesqieu, Baron de. *The Spirit of the Laws*, 1748, Book XIV & Book XIX, Hafner Press, New York, 1949.

Morton, Andrew H & Hayes, John. *Tolkien's Gedling*. Brewin Books, Studley, Warwickshire, 2008.

Nordau, Max Simon. *Degeneration*, General Books, Danvers, Massachusetts, 2009.

Norman, F M. *The Schoolmaster's Drill Assistant, A Manual of Drill for Elementary Schools*, Bemrose & Sons, 6th Edition Revised, London 1873.

Oldfield, E A L. *History of the Army Physical Training Corps*, Gale & Polden, Aldershot, 1955.

Pegg, J Robert. *Quick March! To Athletic Sports, The Origins and Development of Drill, Athletics, Cricket, Football and Swimming in Croydon's Public Elememtary Schools 1893-1910: A Newspaper, Documentary History.* abpublishing, 2011.

Pegg, J Robert. *In Sickness and In Health. The Origins and Systematic Development of Children's Medical Inspection and Treatment in the County of Surrey's Public Elementary Schools 1905-1921 Pioneered by Dr Thomas Henry Jones. A Documentary History*, Vol. 1, abpublishing, 2017

Pegg, J Robert. *In the Swim. The Origins and Systematic Development of Children's Swimming in the County of Surrey's Public Elementary Schools 1905-1921 Pioneered by Major Arthur Ormand Norman. A Documentary History with Various Appendices including Swimming and Washing Verminous Children in the London School Board*. Vol 3, abpublishing, 2017.

Penn, Alan. *Targeting Schools, Drill, Militarism & Imperialism*, Woburn Press, London, 1999.

Plato. *The Republic*, 380 BC, translated by H D P Lee, Penguin Classics, Harmondsworth, 1955.

Plato. *The Laws*, 350 BC, translated by Saunders, Trevor J, Penguin, Harmondsworth, 1970.

Popper, Karl. *The Open Society and Its Enemies, The Spell of Plato*, Volume I, Routledge Kegan & Paul, London, 1945.

Porter, Dorothy. *Health, Civilization and the State*, Routledge, London, 1999.

Porter, Roy. Madness and Its Institutions, in Wear, Andrew, ed. *Medicine In Society*, CUP, 1992.

Puritz, Ludwig. Translated by Knofe, O and MacQueen J W. *Code Book of Gymnastic Exercises*, Kegan, Paul, Trench, Trubner & Co., 3rd Edition, London 1905.

Reeder, D A. ed. *Urban Education in the Nineteenth Century, Proceedings of the 1976 Annual Conference of the History of Education Society of Great Britain*, Taylor & Francis Ltd., London 1977.

Richards, Janet Radcliffe. *Human Nature after Darwin, A Philosophical Introduction*, Routledge, 2000.

Richter, Melvin. *The Politics of Conscience, T H Green and His Age*, University Press of America, Lanham, New York.

Robinson, David. *Surrey Through the Century 1889-1989*, SCC 1989.

Roland, George. *An Introductory Course of Modern Gymnastics*, Oliver & Boyd, Tweedale Court, 1832.

Rousseau, Jean-Jacques, translated by Foxley, Barbara. *Emile,* 1762, Everyman's Library, J M Dent 1974.

Rousseau, Jean-Jacques. translated by Blair, Lowell. *The Essential Rousseau*, Mentor, New American Library, New York, 1974.

SCC. *Handbook for Managers of PES*, SCC, Second Edition, 1912.

Seaborne, Malcolm and Lowe, Roy. *The English School, its architecture and organization*, Volume II 1870-1970, Routledge & Kegan Paul, London 1977.

Searle, G R. *The Quest for National Efficiency, A Study of British Politics and Political Thought 1899-1914*, Basil Blackwell, Oxford, 1971.

Sewell, Dennis. *The Political Gene, How Darwin's ideas Changed Politics*, Picador, London, 2009.

Smith, W. David. *Stretching Their Bodies, The History of Physical Education*, David & Charles, Newton Abbot 1974.

Stewart, W A C. *Progressives and Radicals in English Education 1750-1970*, MacMillan, London 1972.

The Holy Bible, King James Version

Thomson, David. *Europe Since Napolean*, Penguin Books, Harmondsworth, Middlesex, 1966.

Tissot, Joseph-Clement. *Medicinal And Surgical Gymnastics, 1780*, Bastien, Little Lion Street, Paris. Published by Licht, Elizabeth, New Haven, Connecticut, 1964.

Warwick, The Countess of. *A Nation's Youth, Physical Deterioration: Its Causes and Some Remedies*, Cassell & Company, Limited, 1906.

Zweiniger-Bargielowska, Ina. *Managing the Body, Beauty, Health and Fitness in Britain 1880-1939*, OUP, 2010.